A LOVE LETTER
OF LIFE LESSONS

LARISSA PARAS

HERE'S THE THING

A LOVE LETTER OF LIFE LESSONS

LARISSA PARAS

ISBN (Print Edition): 978-1-66787-723-5

ISBN (eBook Edition): 978-1-66787-724-2

To my mom, Violet.

To Nicole, my sounding board.

*To the sisters I chose along the way that
guide, shape, and love me.*

To my teenage self... You're enough. You always were.

Contents

Introduction

In my late teens and early twenties, my goal was to be unique, but not so different that people thought I was weird. I wanted to be successful in everything I did. I wanted to belong. I wanted to have my hands in everything, I wanted to leave my mark. I wanted everyone to like me. I would've done almost anything to not ruffle too many feathers. I always had a passion for "good trouble" and fighting for a cause. I wanted to not care what people thought of the way I looked and dressed, but I did care, deeply. I wanted to stand out while blending in. What can I say? I'm a Gemini and very complex.

"Do it all, all of the time," was what my thirties brought me. I was coming into my own as a wife, mother, veteran teacher, and all of the things that come with being a woman of the world. I was killing myself wearing all of the hats at the same time. I was stretched too thin. I volunteered for far too much. I had a hard time saying no to the needs of my friends, my boss, my children, my husband, and even my own "great ideas." If I had a great idea I couldn't let it alone or save it for later. I would engage in it, make it, plan it, do it… All the while, exhausting myself and not taking care of myself at all. I was overextended. I was losing a sense of who I was. My identity was in all of the hats I was wearing, but I was forgetting who I was in the essence of my being.

I finally woke up to the realization that my exhaustion was because I was choosing this path. I was always putting my needs last and I knew that if I kept going, I'd end up losing all sense of who I was as a person. I would be so tied to the labels of who I was… A teacher, a mother, a wife, that I would forget who LaRissa was and what brought her joy.

I was also watching my beautiful mother's health deteriorate at this time. I watched her struggle to take care of herself because she was focused on doing work for others while sacrificing her physical and mental health. I knew I was on the same path. It was destroying her and breaking my heart. Simultaneously, I was watching friends getting sucked into the "hustle culture" without taking care of themselves at all. I needed to learn from this and change the familiar patterns that I was surrounded by.

My mom has taught me so many great things—how to be compassionate, how to make a house a home, how to give amazing hugs, positivity as a choice, the importance of books and education, and so much more. Watching her struggle by stretching herself too thin, I felt like I was watching her slowly kill herself without even realizing it.

I want to do better, for myself and for my family. I want my kids to learn boundaries, and I need to lead by example. I want to be the mom that still moves around easily and plays, regardless of her age. I want to be a wife that has the energy to give to her husband, instead of putting him at the bottom of the list. I want to be the teacher that loves her job and not be the one that grows into the curmudgeon that people are excited to see retire.

I needed to learn how to say no. I needed to learn when to say yes. I needed to learn how to be present. I needed to learn to take healthy risks. I needed to learn to let go of toxic people. I needed to learn how to connect with myself and my heart and my joy again. I needed to learn how to take better care of myself. I needed to remember to have fun once in a while! And I did. I'm still learning and doing the work to improve myself FOR MYSELF.

I had to really stop and listen to my heart and my body. This book is full of the lessons that I've learned. Following the lessons will take listening to your inner voice and paying attention to your body's reactions; reflecting and being honest with yourself; being brave enough to follow through; believing you're worth fighting for; respecting and loving yourself so hard that you don't allow people into your inner circle that don't love and respect you. These are the lessons that I don't have time to teach in a history class but that are vital to our personal journeys. It's also a love letter to my younger self. I need her to know that we are grown, safe, and making great progress. (Everyone writes a book to heal her inner child, right?!)

Here's the thing... In order to begin, begin.

PART 1:

Relationship with Ourselves

Dear You,

Oh, beautiful human. I see you over there, obsessing over every morsel that passes through your lips. Bodies are not supposed to look like only one thing. Listen to what your body needs and go from there. Thank your body for all it does. Treat it well. Your body is not the enemy.

Love, LP

P.S. Your mantra.. I have gratitude for my body. xo

Is My Body Bad?

I was the proudest fifth grader in a training bra that you'd ever seen. It was an ivory flower print racerback, and I felt like a big deal. I felt like I had arrived! 1986 was going to be a great year! We had a new girl in our class that year, and she remembers her first day partly because of me and this bra. I loudly whispered to every girl about my new bra while wearing a T-shirt that had frogs in a row boat labeled "Toadly Oarsome" (pure 80s). I was stoked to be a budding woman and to start my initiation into this mysterious club of wonder—until boys started snapping my bra. Suddenly I was uncomfortable in my body and eventually my self-esteem began to erode.

Then came middle school. I joined the cheerleading team, tried my hand at volleyball (I treated this like a duck and cover drill), and even performed with a group of other girls to the retro hit "Rock Around the Clock" for our school talent show. We lost. I had a crush on a boy named Chris. I held hands with Greg, but I would not let him kiss me. I wanted to be grown up, but I was NOT ready. It was sometime during these middle school years that my chest size bypassed my mom's. I wondered if my boobs would ever stop growing.

Next was high school. I heard my uncle make comments about me being a "loose cheerleader." The assumption was that because I was a cheerleader I MUST be easy. Because I had a 36C in middle school must mean I'm sexually active. And then the locker room was a new thing for us girls. Most of us were modest, but I did notice my chest was larger than most. And the breasts that were supposed to make me feel like a woman just felt like gross balls of fat. I had been excited about wearing a bra, but then it felt like an embarrassment to me. I started to be ashamed of my body—my body that had done nothing wrong but grow the way it's supposed to. Sometimes I thought my boobs "made me look slutty." I did not want that reputation. I tried to hide them with baggy shirts and minimizing bras. At one point, I taped them down to smash them into submission. Anything to not attract unwanted attention. I felt like my blossoming body didn't match how I felt on the inside.

As I matured I was less embarrassed by my breasts, and even started celebrating their existence in college. But there was a part that felt like they were still just in the way. The relationship that I had with my body was becoming increasingly challenging. I wanted to embrace being feminine and a woman, but I felt like every time I did, I was also getting attention from people who were making me feel uncomfortable.

Loving our bodies is hard when we feel like we are getting so many messages about what they should look like and how the world places different values on different types. It's confusing as a kid, and it's confusing as an adult. We get a lot of mixed messages. Love your body, but not so much that it pushes people away. All bodies are beautiful, but you should buy "these" products to make you thinner, clearer, and younger. Fight fat! Fight wrinkles! Fight cellulite! This hyper-consumerism is exhausting.

Companies feed off of our insecurities to sell their products and make a buck. But where does that lead us? Let's dig into that.

From my experience, women tend to criticize themselves too much over their outer appearance. We compare ourselves to something computer-generated too often, and our young ones are seeing it and doing the same. Let's change the conversation to how to be good people, how to be our best selves, how to embrace our talents, strengths, and creativity, and how to treat ourselves and those around us well.

And let's be clear that this conversation isn't just about women. Our young men see the same images in the media as our young women do. The insane expectations that we have for each other can be overwhelming and unobtainable. If most of the images we see of men are "bumbling fun idiots," "hyper-masculine," "ragey, body builders," or "power sharks," then that is what young women will expect out of our young men. If most of the images we see for women are "sex kittens," "dumb and pretty," or "bitches," then that is what young men will expect out of our young women. If we only ever see stereotypes of certain races or LGBTQ+ people then we will expect these behaviors and not see the whole person. We need to be aware of this. These messages really keep everyone in a box and are making it hard for people to reach their full potential.

In order to love our bodies more, we need to invest in changing our mindset about them. This takes time and work but is so important to breaking the cycle of how we talk to ourselves and how we talk about others. And here's the thing… It starts with us. How we talk to ourselves and about each other matters. How we spend our money and who we give our energy to matters. Our attention is a commodity in the media world these days. Companies make money on every ad, story, and post you click on and engage with. Like any great change we want to make, it needs to start with ourselves and our circles.

This section is going to give you so many ideas to get going in the right direction. And here's the thing: it all starts with you.

A Bathing Suit Body

I bought my first bikini for spring break of my sophomore year of high school. My best friend, Michele, had invited me to join her family in Florida, and I was so pumped for this adventure! It was my first trip to a warm, tropical place, and I couldn't contain my excitement! Choosing outfits with my mom for the trip became my mission for the month leading up to the blessed spring break event. I come from a chilly little northern town, and we landed at one of the golf and ski resort shops to find our new spring break suits. It was there that I found a Jag multi-colored fluorescent bikini. The first best part was that my boobs actually fit into it, and I didn't look like a playboy centerfold with her tiny triangle top. The second-best part that I discovered later, was that the bottom didn't ride up, giving me a constant wedgie. I still love a two-piece for this reason. Between the DDs and a long torso, a tank suit is always riding up my butt!

So, fast forward twenty-five years and two children later. I still love a bikini but feel way less confident in one. I'm not as toned as I used to be, I have thick thighs and a muffin top. Basically, I'm a regular woman and not a supermodel. And this is okay, acceptable, and wonderful, even.

Last summer, I was getting ready to take the kids to the beach and started an internal debate about wearing a one-piece or two-piece bathing suit. I heard my own voice say, as it has said to many other women, "If you have a body and you have a bikini, you have a bikini body." So, I threw it on. If I sat still, tightening my buried abs, it would look okay. In my mind, I also heard my friend, Sonja, telling me to wear it and that I was beautiful. Critics be damned! But I was still nervous. Whatever. We were running late so I threw on one of my husband's old button-down shirts and some shorts and schlepped the kids to the beach. I was going to be OK. I was only going to be sitting on the beach.

Fast forward an hour later: the kids were doing beach things, and I was working on this book, journal in hand. Child One was playing frisbee and asked if I would play with him. Immediately, I panicked on the inside. I would be standing up, moving my body, and doing it in front of total strangers. Without the safety of the blanket and beach chair. My pale doughy stomach, exposed to the world. Every lump and jiggle out there for the busy beach to see. I did not want to get up. I wanted to say no. But something else inside me started speaking. There was a part of me that wanted to play and not give a care about not being a model. I might not feel comfortable, but I was going to be alright. My body is part of me and my truth. So that day, that second part of me won, and I played frisbee with my boy. Right out there in the open, my mom-body was catching and tossing a frisbee. And here's the thing, once I got going, when I wasn't thinking about how I might look and what was jiggling or not, I was actually enjoying myself—and hanging out with my cool, teenage son! And he didn't care about the way my body looked. He was happy to play!

I have watched too many of my peers sit on the sidelines and not enjoy time with their kids because of the shame surrounding their bodies in bathing suits. I certainly have before, and thinking about this makes me really sad. Child One and I had a lovely time that day. We laughed and acted silly. If I had let my fear, shame, and self-loathing keep me on that beach towel, I never would've had that time with him. Looking back, I wonder how many moments I've missed already because of the shame around my body.

Stepping into our bathing suits is harder some days than it is others. Different seasons in life have us looking different than we used to. Our bodies do some amazing things and it's okay if we don't look like an airbrushed glossy magazine model or a filtered Instagram influencer. I'll admit, I'm usually worried about my thighs and my squishy tummy area, but here's the thing—and this is the WORK—we need to recognize the non-productive talk in our heads and flip the script. Instead of judgment, remember the good.

My legs are strong.

My body carried two healthy babies.

I'm able to think and learn.

My lungs are breathing.

My heart is pumping.

I can give love.

I can receive love.

I can't let my worry about what others think or old shame about my body prevent me from living. I want to throw a frisbee on the beach. I want to play catch. I want to hike, dance, and do yoga. And I can! I can do all of these things and I don't have to look like a supermodel to do them; I can just look like me, a forty-something woman. And getting into this mindset involves a lot of reflection, some good therapy, working on my personal development, and letting go of the negative stuff. And it's totally doable! So, my wish for you right now is that you can start to enjoy yourself and appreciate yourself as wonderful as you are. Remember to speak kindly to yourself and your body, as if it were a good friend because it is. And it's the only one you get. Love her like the goddess she is.

Fat isn't a Feeling

I was in my early thirties before I genuinely felt enjoyment and love toward my body. I spent a lot of time before that being very uncomfortable in my own skin. When I was a little girl, I very much loved my body and all the things I could do. I could run and play, and I was very bendy. I could dance and I could jump, and even if I wasn't winning games or races, I didn't care; I was having fun. But at some point, I started to feel uncomfortable with my body. I started to "feel fat." I feel sympathy now for the girl that lost herself in that attitude for decades, but proud that I have finally had some clarity and revelation when it comes to my body. I feel bad for those times when I was so uncomfortable and ashamed that I tried to turn myself into something that I wasn't. Ping-ponging between fad diets and overeating. Both left me feeling unsuccessful, empty, and in a constant state of unworthiness.

I thought about my weight and my body constantly. I tried to get it to transform into a six-foot-tall hundred-pound supermodel. This was impossible! I'm 5'4 ½" and naturally curvy. I saw lovely images on TV, in movies, and in magazines and it made me feel "less than." I compared my body shape and size to that of my classmates and my friends. And even when I was forty pounds smaller than I am right now, I felt like the largest girl on my team. I was desperate to gain the attention of boys to feel validated. I spent several years as an on and off again bulimic. I felt like if I could punish my body enough it would submit to thinness.

I thought being thin was being healthy. Looking back, at my smallest, I was my least healthy.

When I was shaming my body in the worst ways, I really had no idea I was doing it. And I don't think I'm alone. I see and hear women constantly talk poorly about themselves.

Here's how we shame our bodies:

- By comparing ourselves to others.

- By saying shitty things to our bodies, like "fat ass."

- By believing advertising. Remember, marketing is designed to make us always want more by feeling "less than." (Marketing is supposed to make you want to invest in a certain product or idea. That's its JOB. It's your job as a CONSUMER to be thoughtful and strategic with what you buy. And to tell the body shamers—like the ones trying to sell you weight loss tea on IG because they say you're not thin enough—to suck it.)

- By constantly complaining about our bodies to our friends and daughters. (It's also teaching them to start hating their bodies, thus continuing the cycle).

- By starving our bodies.

- By stuffing our bodies with unhealthy processed food, day in and day out, as comfort.

- By taking pills to change them to look a certain way. (I'm not talking about a multivitamin or a good supplement for something that helps you. I'm talking about those things that make you feel jittery. Don't buy your health care products from a gas station!).

- By over-exercising and undereating. (Exercise is VITAL! Of course, we all need to move our bodies, but I'm talking about OBSESSING over it.).

- By expecting perfection in ourselves and others at all times.

When I was younger, I was so focused on the parts I didn't like about myself that it never occurred to me that someone else might be envious of some of those parts. For example, I was blessed with a substantial chest. But early on, I was embarrassed by this. My body drew a lot of unwanted attention and comments from boys and men. At one point, I started taping them up with masking tape to flatten them out. One night in college, I was complaining about my giant boobs with a group of girlfriends. My super cute friend, Becky, who was small-chested, told me how she felt bad because she DIDN'T have big boobs. She told me that she was made fun of for looking like a little boy and that sometimes she wished she had a rack like mine. I was blown away. I had never thought that someone small and perfect in my eyes might not like something about herself. The fact that we were both made to feel uncomfortable with our chests is a story for another book.

I spent years listening to women criticize other women about their shapes and sizes. Like "so-and-so has gained a lot of weight." Or asking, "Am I as fat as that lady?" or "Make sure I don't get as big as her." I also grew up with a beautiful, thin mother who was always saying how fat she was. When I heard these words, they seeped into my psyche. I KNOW that this was not my mother's intention. But, I think subconsciously I felt nervous that if I weren't perfect, or small enough, then I wouldn't be lovable. I wouldn't be worthy.

I also remember watching my beautiful aunties talking about their diets and celebrating weight loss and not understanding why they were so hard on themselves. I admired them and loved them for who they were not for their sizes and shapes. Of course, I wanted them to be healthy and happy; I just didn't want them to force themselves into a mold that wasn't theirs. That's what I want for myself now. To be comfortable in my skin and less judgmental about my body.

I still struggle with how I feel toward my body. (In my first draft of this book, I kept referring to my body as "it" like something that was not actually ME. I had to go back and edit those to say "I.") Learning to love yourself and continuing to do so is a lifelong process. It doesn't happen overnight but it's one of the greatest things you can do for yourself and for the people around you.

Let me explain.

When you start loving yourself—genuinely showing yourself compassion—you will start showing more love and compassion to those around you, and vice versa. When you start to become conscious of how often you're judging and shaming yourself and start changing your inner dialog, you will feel calmer, and less anxious. You'll also start to become more aware of the negative self-talk in your friends and call them out on it in a loving way. You'll start to have meaningful conversations around health. And maybe when you were silently judging and shaming yourself, you were talking about other women behind their backs (or judging the looks and shapes of other women). Through the act of self-compassion you'll start to be kinder and less judgmental of others and the struggles they might have. When I hated my body the most, I also found myself discussing so-and-so and HER body changes—good or bad—to others. The body shaming cycle continued even outside of myself. I was pushing my insecurities out in the form of judging others.

When I catch myself saying "I feel fat" these days I stop myself and say, "fat is not a feeling. What is really going on?"

Some other "feels" I'm actually feeling:

- I feel bloated. I'll drink more water and eat more veg to feel better.

- I'm disappointed that my pants feel tight this week.

- I feel ashamed because I've been comparing myself to others. I need to focus on the good stuff and the things I am thankful for.
- I just enjoyed a really special celebration. Permission granted to enjoy myself. Please don't feel guilty about celebrating and enjoying a delicious meal.

I would love to see a world where we valued HEALTH over just being thin. Healthy can be a size eighteen or a size four. That's something for you and your doctor to talk about. Do not let a fad diet or a health blogger determine that for you. And just because someone is smokin' hot on IG doesn't mean they're a health expert. Just because someone is famous doesn't make them an expert either.

And in the spirit of being completely transparent here, I have had to LEARN how to treat my body in healthier ways—physically and mentally. I had to learn to love myself more so I could take better care of myself. I've had to learn to give myself grace with my imperfections. This is work, but I did it because when I was treating myself better by eating better and moving in ways that felt good to me I felt better, physically and emotionally. More plants, more lean proteins, less processed food, and more water, and I've had to learn to listen to my body. If it hurts to eat it or drink it, it's not for me. I've had to break up with beer and some dairy in the past few years. (It's okay, they understood "it's not you, it's me", and the universe gave me wine, hard cider, and oat milk. It's all good.)

How Do You Love Your Body?

"TO LOVE YOURSELF IS
A NEVER-ENDING PROCESS."
- Oprah Winfrey

We've all heard it a million times; all bodies and sizes are beautiful. But, sometimes what we hear and see are two different things. We see thin, fit, clear-skinned, smooth-haired women and they grace our screens and glossy magazines. We often see beautiful women in our own lives complaining constantly about their stomachs, skin, noses, chins, cheeks, wrinkles, bums… And the list goes on. We see surgically enhanced features and filters and photoshopped bodies all the time.

If you're like me, you know that the phrase "my body is a temple" comes in waves. I'd like to think that by now, at forty-something, this is how I treat myself the majority of the time. But, in my twenties… rarely. Even now, I go through weeks where I don't drink enough water and eat far too many pastries.

One morning, I was up early running with my pal, Megan, and felt my belly shake in a way that made me cringe on the inside and say out loud, "I'm such a fat ass! My gut is BOUNCING!" Then I immediately thought, 'I'm not practicing what I preach. I shouldn't talk like that to myself. I wouldn't say things to my friends or family like that. Why would I say them to myself?' And then proceeded to feel guilty for trashing myself. (My inner dialog is like a really weird Twitter feed sometimes.)

As the day went on, I decided that rather than hating on myself for BEING AN IMPERFECT HUMAN LIKE EVERYONE ELSE, I would treat myself better and not expect perfection. This was an attitude shift. I was very conscious of my actions toward myself, both physically and mentally, and honestly, I was really trying to give myself the nurturing that I preach about to my children and students.

So, how do we love our bodies better amongst all of this noise? It comes down to our minds. We need to develop the mental muscle.

First, we need to be aware of the negative self-talk. We need to call ourselves out on it; personally, and with our friends. My friend, Joyce, is really good at this. She's great at flipping the script and encouraging the people around her to do it, too.

Be conscious that when we tell lies like "I'm ugly," "I hate my chin" or "I'm such a fat ass," we are really telling ourselves we're not good enough or not worthy enough. Being aware that this is crushing our hearts and self-esteem, we can take the next step: changing our dialogue.

Instead of "I am fat" or whatever negative thought you tell yourself about your body, thank your body for doing all it does for you. Thank your body for walking, going to work, putting a Band-Aid on the baby, creating a spreadsheet, writing an essay, breathing, waking up, and taking care of all the things that matter to us. Be grateful for what your body does for you, and acknowledge that it does so much.

Thank your body for breathing, thank it for speaking, thank it for lifting things, thank it for digesting your food, thank it for anything and everything. It sounds a little cheesy, right? I'm with you. But here's the thing; whatever words you feed your mind, you'll start to believe them. Many of us, for years, have believed the negative. So, feed your mind with gratitude and compassion. Think about it like this: would you say nasty things to your best friend or to your child? No, I don't think you would. So why are you saying them to yourself?

Loving your body, thus loving yourself, is a lifelong process. It ebbs and flows depending on which season we're in. We need to remember to be patient with ourselves. Being perfect should never be the goal. Making positive progress is a much more admirable goal. Being brave enough to move away from negative behaviors, situations, and people will help you move in the right direction. Remember, it's all a journey. Learning to love your body and continuing to do so is a journey. Be kind to yourself.

Now, just like anything, this isn't a habit that's easy to acquire. It takes time and practice.

Here are some things that help. They're not always easy, but it's important work.

1. Make a list of ten things you like about yourself. Hang this list where you can see it daily. Read it often. Revise it sometimes.

2. Look in the mirror. Really look at yourself. Look at the details. Send each of your parts love. Look at the sparkle in your eyes; the way you hold your head. Send love to your lungs for helping you breathe, and your eyes for seeing beauty. Send love to your mouth for speaking your truth and being

brave. Thank your hands for helping you to create. Send love to your legs for supporting you, etc.

3. Wear clothes you like, in the correct size. You'll feel better and look better.

4. Do fun activities that you love, regardless of your size. Love to dance? DANCE! Love to do karate? DO IT! Don't stop doing what you love because of what you think you look like on the outside.

5. Spend time with people that focus more on LIVING life, instead of people who are obsessed with their size and shape.

6. Remind yourself that you are BEAUTIFUL the way you are. You were created to do amazing things.

7. Move your body in a way that makes you feel good… in ways that make you feel centered, strong, flexible, and energized. Make these things routine.

8. Practice tuning in to your body. Rest when you're tired. Eat when you're hungry. Move your body when you need it.

9. Remember that what you see on TV, in magazines, and online shows a lot of "perfection" and photo editing. No one is perfect and most celebs have whole teams making them look a certain way. Find real role models in the real world, too.

10. Get creative. Draw, cook, craft, write… CREATE.

11. Get outside. Spend some time unplugged and in nature.

12. Make "I am enough, just as I am" your new mantra. Make yourself a sign and post it up as a reminder.

13. Inner light is not a myth. Think about your favorite people to be around. You enjoy them for how they treat you, how they make you feel, and how you feel around them. You don't care if they wear the latest trends or have on a full face of makeup. You like their spirit and are drawn to their light.

Toxic Positivity
& Sitting with the Suck

Is there such a thing as being too positive? Without question, yes. Toxic positivity is when you are excessive and overly optimistic in all situations. When you maintain this optimism at all costs, you can deny yourself and invalidate your true human experiences and emotions. If you never sit with uncomfortable feelings, if you always push those things down, you'll never deal with them. And they always bubble back up at inopportune times. That's not to say that you shouldn't have a good attitude and you shouldn't be positive. What I'm saying is that it's okay to acknowledge emotions like anger, disappointment, and sadness.

It's okay to look for the light at the end of the tunnel, but it's also important to live through the suckiness of the tunnel itself. The journey we call life isn't always rainbows and sunshine. Sometimes life is rocky and hard. It's important to acknowledge all of the negative emotions that we're often told to get rid of because they're uncomfortable. Talking about going through the struggle will make completing the final goals we have so much more fulfilling. I think it's in our human nature to distract ourselves when things are uncomfortable and unpleasant. It's the way our body protects itself. But being vulnerable is being brave, and being brave will help you reach your full potential and authentic spirit.

Having hard conversations that feel confrontational is my least favorite type of conversation. I can be a master at avoiding them, and I've had years of practice. My go-to tactic was to keep myself busy doing anything, so I wouldn't have to have the conversation. My house was never cleaner.

These days I have learned to talk to myself first; to ask questions and listen to my gut for answers. Here's how I would start: ask yourself why you're feeling the way you are. Really get in there. Peel back the layers. Ask yourself why over and over again.

- Nervous about setting boundaries? Why don't you want to make the phone call? Are you such a people pleaser that the thought of disappointing someone makes you sick?

- Pissed off? Are you mad because the kid didn't pick up their socks or are you upset because you feel unheard all of the time?

- Feeling restless? Holding still makes you feel anxious? Are you worried people will think you're lazy?

When you have really sat with the negative feelings, that's when you can make a real plan to move forward in a way that feels good to you. Your body is built to have emotions, just like it's built to breathe and digest and make your heart beat. The problem sometimes is that our brains and thoughts get in the way of us having our emotions. You are not made of Teflon. You are allowed to be sad, mad, sick, and hurt. Listen to your body. Don't discredit what it's telling you. The body holds so much information if we really stop and listen.

Toxic positivity can also be pushed onto others. When you say things like "it is what it is" or "it could always be worse," or just send feel-good quotes to people you are inadvertently shaming them for expressing anything but happiness. You are minimizing their experience instead of validating their emotions.

You can still be supportive by validating how someone is feeling and offering up support. (Maybe even tweaking the words a little when you need to talk to yourself, too.)

- That is stressful. How can I help?

- Do you want to brainstorm solutions or would you just like me to listen?

- This is really hard. I'm thinking of you.

- I see you and I am here for you.

- You are not alone.

- This sucks. I'm sorry you're going through this.

- How can I support you?

Being a healthy human involves being mindful of how we show up in the world. If you are a transmitter of toxic positivity, you are hurting yourself and the people around you. Try to find balance in your emotions instead of an all-or-nothing mentality. It starts with awareness.

Self-Care and Self-Compassion

Change in life is inevitable. For life events, for the world, and for our bodies. But how we react to the change will make all of the difference between being happy and being miserable—the difference between finding joy and purpose and staying stuck.

Self-care and self-compassion are two trending phrases that I didn't specifically define for myself until I was in my forties.

I had always thought that when people said self-care, they meant go spend a lot of money and spend the day at the spa. First of all, I didn't have the budget for a day at the spa. Second, laying still for a massage when I had a to-do list the length of my arm sounded like torture to my workaholic-anxiety-riddled self. But I knew I wasn't taking care of myself, and I honestly felt like I didn't even know how.

A wise woman reminded me what self-care is really all about. It's just about taking care of yourself the way you would take care of another creature that you loved. Think of this: what if the most adorable dog or cat showed up on your front porch? She is cold, hungry, dirty, and scared. How would you take care of her? You'd probably start with her basic needs, right? You'd give her a good meal and fresh water. You'd give her a bath and give her a cozy spot to rest. You wouldn't immediately demand tricks or some sort of performance. You would first want her to feel safe and rested.

Friends, that's how you first need to take care of yourself, too. Self-care isn't about heading to the spa, although that could be part of it. First, it's about looking at your basic needs. This is not selfish. This is healthy and sets a good example for the people around you. As we get older, remember that QUALITY matters. If you can control the quality of your life, why wouldn't you do that? Here are some simple self-care questions to get started.

- When was the last time you fueled your body with healthy food?
- How much water have you had today?
- Do you need to rest? Do it, I give you permission. You can't run on an empty tank.
- How was your hygiene? Take some time to let the water roll all over you.

- Do you need some movement to get more oxygen into your bloodstream?

"When anxiety is up, self-care is down." This quote has stuck with me now for a couple of years. It rings true for me most of the time. If I start to feel anxious, I ask myself those questions above. Usually, I have neglected myself in one of these ways. If I can start to add those basics of self-care into my life and be present with them, I can usually stave off a full-blown panic attack down the road.

So, if self-care is more physical and emotional care, then self-compassion is the stuff going on inside of your head. Self-compassion is being aware of your inner dialogue and how it's affecting the way you feel about yourself.

We've often heard things about ourselves that somehow get "stuck" in our subconscious. It might be about our body, our abilities, how smart we are, where we are from, our sexuality, or any number of things. Often these turn into a negative dialogue that we start to believe. Sometimes we believe these lies for DECADES. Sometimes the shame we have holds us back from being open to love, and even loving ourselves.

When I was in middle and high school I was a cheerleader. The stereotypes surrounding cheerleaders were generally not kind—things like ditzy, slutty, and stupid. I felt like I had to constantly prove to the world that I was not a dumb whore. I heard these things from classmates and grown adults. I had an uncle that thought this was the funniest thing to say about cheerleading to me. I had a hard time embracing my own sexuality because of all of the shame and stigma around this. I struggled with feeling ashamed when I didn't feel smart enough. I struggled between being "too much" and not enough. It's something that still pops up in my head decades later. I've had to learn compassion for myself in these moments.

Having compassion for yourself is like treating yourself the way you would treat a good friend. You would never expect perfection from her. You would never call her names. You would never belittle her dreams. You would encourage her. You would remind her of all of her beautiful qualities. You would thank her for all she does for you. You would shut down that negative talk she says about being dumb, out of shape, and unsure. You would help her find some positive affirmations to repeat daily; you would help her make a list of things she does well and likes about herself. You would help her generate a gratitude list. You'd help her set goals that look to her future dreams. You would be an excellent friend to her.

You need to be an excellent friend to yourself. That is self-compassion.

Start here:

Taking care of yourself isn't just getting your monthly cut, color, and wax. You've got to take care of your basics, physically and mentally. If it's too hard, you need to possibly seek out a professional therapist to help you retrain yourself. If we can take our self-care and self-compassion seriously, we can start to become more full, whole, and happy. We can stop dreaming and start working on our goals to make our dreams a reality. When we practice these things, we are leading by example for the others around us, and then maybe, they'll start this journey too.

5 Positive Affirmations   5 Gratitudes

Self Compassion

5 Things I am Proud Of   5 Dreams

Health is so Much More than a Number

For a very long time, I associated thinness with health. It was so ingrained in my teenage brain that I actually did some of the unhealthiest things to try to achieve that skinny goal. During a period of my life when I felt like I was trapped in a body that could never live up to the expectations I saw in my head as "perfect," I developed an eating disorder. I was trying to gain control over things I could not control. Later, I learned to rise up and to ask for professional help and I eventually got myself back.

Here's the thing: healthy bodies can have a lot of different shapes. Genetics are a factor. You and your doctors want to be the ones to look at your specific skill range for your unique body. (This is the part where I give you the disclaimer that I'm not a medical professional… But I had a couple of medical professionals look at this and they gave me the thumbs up.)

I have done a lot of self-improvement work in my life so far, and it's something that I enjoy because it feels good to me. I'm super curious about the brain-body connection. The research is starting to catch up with what I've felt in my body for decades. We have the power to change our processes to better our lives. When I was in high school, I was on a state championship competitive cheer team. One of the practices our coach wanted us to do was to visualize ourselves doing our routines in our minds before bed. If we made a mistake, we were to start over. I found myself learning our routines better and my muscle memory improving with both the physical repetitions at practice and in the mental ones before bed.

Then I discovered yoga. My first class was through a community education program where we met in a high school classroom. I don't remember my instructor's name, but he was soft-spoken and knew a lot about yoga and energy. He was a true Yogi, not a gym rat. After the first class, I left feeling more connected to myself than maybe I ever had before. I felt strong, calm, and present. I felt an energy in and around myself that I cultivated when my body and mind were in sync. I was hooked. I'm proud to say that I've been practicing for over twenty-five years and even earned my yoga teaching certification. I make time for regular practice, but I also turn to my mat during periods of high stress. It grounds me and centers me in a way that nothing else can. I even pray best this way; moving my body to focus my mind.

So, when we think about health, we need to make sure we are thinking about more than just our caloric intake or how many times a week we go for a run. Be mindful of all the pieces that work together to make us wholly healthy. They are all important to our overall health and well-being.

To take care of our health, fully we need to think about these five aspects:

- Movement
- Fuel
- Sleep
- Spirit
- Reflection

These five things don't just take into account our physical bodies, but our mental health and emotional well-being, too. Let's break them down.

MOVEMENT

Exercise is so important for so many reasons! It improves your body's stress response, lowers the risk for some diseases, tones muscle, burns fat, and boosts your mood. The Mayo Clinic (2021) recommends that adults work in a minimum of 150 minutes of moderate aerobic activity (movement that gets your heart rate up for a bit) into their lives per week. I think that sometimes we get hung up on the word "exercise," especially those of us that have always felt a little unathletic. Or some of us try to do the workouts that are trendy or the ones that we think we SHOULD do. We might try some trend, hate it, give up, and tell ourselves the lie that we're not the "workout type". But here's the thing: everyone has something they like. You just need to find your thing. Think about how you moved your body as a kid and try a similar adult activity. I loved dancing as a kid, so Pilates feels like ballet to me. And taking a dance class for grown-ups every so often has been fun. There are tons of free lessons for both of these online. I'm not a great runner, but I love a good long walk, and with a walk, I only have to change my shoes after work, not my entire outfit. Yay! And yoga to me is both physical and spiritual, so two birds with one stone!

Another great thing to think about is sneaking in extra movement throughout the day. Try:

- Parking further out in the parking lot.

- Taking the stairs.

- Taking walking break laps at work or school.

- Set up walking dates to catch up with friends. Either in person or on the phone. Entertainment while you move your body!

- Walking around the couch when the ads pop up.

FUEL

What you put into your body fuels you. It is recommended by doctors and nutritionists that half of what you consume daily should be fruits and vegetables. The other half should be lean meats, whole grains, and good fats. Limit processed foods and added sugars/sweeteners. You should drink half of your weight in ounces of water daily. (For example, if you weigh 140 pounds, you should be drinking seventy ounces of water per day). Food helps give you energy to accomplish tasks. If you choose to fill your body with more negative things, it can have a negative impact on your body and mind. Too much sugar can make you feel scattered and/or sluggish. Not enough water can lead to headaches and constipation. Out in the world, you will encounter many fad diets and weight loss gimmicks that aren't sustainable. And some aren't even healthy or good for your body. Start to become more mindful of what you eat. And learn some tricks to help yourself thrive in this area. There are a ton of sound nutrition resources out there without following some fad.

When I was a teenager and into my early twenties, I would tell myself that I'd never be thin, which at the time, I equated to being healthy. When I was first learning to fuel my body better, I frequently "fell off the wagon" and beat myself up about it. I spoke harshly to myself saying things like, "I have no willpower," or "I can't do it." Instead of offering myself grace at being an imperfect human striving to be healthy. Eventually, I learned some things that still help me out today.

- Be gentle with yourself. If you make mistakes you're not proud of, remember tomorrow is a new day to try again. Recognize when you are shaming yourself. Speak kindly to yourself the way you would to your friends.

- Celebrate your wins. Beat your water goal? WOOHOO! Drank herbal tea before bed instead of a cookie? Celebrate!

- Keep a food journal. This will help you be accountable to yourself. It will also help you reflect on the patterns that you have.

- Plan ahead. If I plan my meals ahead of time, I'll eat healthier. If I don't, I find myself starving and staring into the pantry. This usually ends up with macaroni and cheese from the box. Too often.

- Try new recipes. I like to follow healthy bloggers and check out library books for new recipe ideas.

SLEEP

I spent my twenties and thirties burning the candle at both ends and staying up late to do it. Sometimes it was to party, watch a movie marathon or to finish writing a paper I had been procrastinating on. Then it was to lesson plan, grade papers, or binge something on Netflix. My bedtime hovered around midnight for decades and most of the time, I was getting up around five AM for work. Factor in the years of children having ear infections and crying through the night, I'm surprised I was a functioning human at all.

The truth is, I wasn't. I was successful by all outward appearances, yes, but I was not physically or mentally healthy.

I was always just keeping busy to be busy. Keeping busy to prove that I could do it all! Sure, everything was done for everyone, but I had forgotten about me. I forgot how to take care of myself in this one way that would help me function better all day—a restful night's sleep.

Here's what sleep does for you:

- It helps your body repair and recover.

- It boosts your immune system. You'll get sick less often.

- It helps you maintain a healthy weight.

- It lowers stress levels.

- It improves your mood.

- It can lower your risk of diabetes and heart disease.

- It improves memory and can help you think clearly - this helps for school and work!

- It can increase physical performance.

Here's how I get mindful about sleep; doing these things is important, especially during times of high stress when sleep might not come as easily. Find a routine that works for you.

- Choose a smart bedtime that follows the natural rhythms of nature. I like to start by counting back from when I need to get up; six to eight hours is recommended for adults.

- Put away small screens like phones and laptops two hours before bed.

- Remove the tv from the bedroom.

- Do not sleep with your phone in the bedroom. That's right. Invest in an old-school alarm clock.

- Herbal tea.

- Nighttime yoga—ten minutes on YouTube, you'll thank me later.

- Reading for fun. This is the thing that calms my monkey mind.

- Keep a pad of paper near your bed to jot down lists or what is on your mind without worrying about forgetting it by morning.

- Create a ritual that takes you away from the screen and gets you ready for the next day like packing a lunch or choosing your outfit.

Sleep is so important, and we don't often give it the credit it deserves. Start today by taking inventory of what you currently do, and create your own list of rituals. It's a smart habit that will help you your whole life and is well worth investing in.

SPIRIT

When I think about nurturing my spirit, I think about the things that call to me, make me feel content, and create a sense of groundedness in my heart. I find this nurturing of spirit in a variety of ways these days, but the hardest thing about trying to find it was to hold still long enough to listen to my body, mind, and heart.

In order to connect to my spirit, I first had to connect to myself by myself. I had to shut out the expectations of the world and what everyone else wanted me to be. I had to think about what really lit me up, made me feel whole, and like MYSELF.

In the hustle and bustle of our world, we sometimes need to be really intentional about nurturing our soul, otherwise, we lose sight of our voice and who we really are because we're working so hard to fit into what society wants us to be.

So, how do we do this? We need to reflect on what brings us joy. When do we feel like our true selves? When was the last time? When do we feel like our light is shining? When do we feel connected? Answer those questions and then carve out the time to actually make your own contentment. It will be unique to you and to your mood.

The first time I ever really felt my energy, my connectedness to God and/or the Universe, I was at a youth retreat in high school. I was sitting alone on the grass near the water. I was either praying or writing and just listening to the sounds around me. I was feeling the sun on my face. I felt a wash of calm over me, and I knew I was part of something greater than myself in this world. My energy was strong, and I knew I would be able to recreate this sensation again. I have found great solace and strength in many places throughout the years. My yoga mat is one of them. A walk in nature, water… oceans, rivers, or my native Great Lakes. In prayer, with old friends, writing, drawing and being creative, or listening to the right music.

Others might connect to their spirits by running, or perched high up in a deer blind, reading inspirational text, baking, making music, dancing, fishing, or meditation. Find your connection to your heart and make time for it frequently.

REFLECTION

There came a point in my mid-thirties when I realized that I'd been avoiding reflection because sometimes it was hard. Not hard in the sense that writing was hard for me to do, but FEELINGS were hard for me to acknowledge. Past hurts were uncomfortable to look back on, and, if I'm being honest, looking at the moments that I was embarrassed or ashamed isn't pleasant to revisit either.

I also felt like I was always too busy to journal and reflect. And I was busy; there's no doubt. Teacher, mentor, wife, and mother; I was burning the midnight oil to keep up with the choices I was making. I was also avoiding any opportunity to think and process my feelings, or my life.

But, when I started journaling more frequently, I felt better. I could get things off my chest. Sometimes, I would just list things I was grateful for. Some things became part of this book.

We are constantly posting, tagging, status updating, tweeting, and on and on and on. We don't often write and reflect for the sake of getting into our own heads. Writing—in a judgment-free, typos-don't-count, let-loose kind of way—is a great way to connect with yourself and to process feelings.

Research tells us that journaling can help us reduce stress, boost our moods, process emotional events, and reduce symptoms of anxiety. And remember, it's for you. Spelling doesn't count.

Here are some great prompts to get you started:

- I am proud of…
- I admire… because…
- If I could go anywhere in the world, I would go to _____ because…
- What have I overcome in my life so far?
- If I could go back and give my younger self some advice, I would tell her…
- If I weren't afraid, I would…
- The most important thing to me is …
- When I'm overwhelmed, I could…
- My favorite quote is …
- Right now, I need …
- I'm proud of myself for …
- I want to forgive …
- I'm frustrated by …
- I'm truly inspired by …
- The nicest compliment I ever received was …
- I would like to see …
- I secretly wish I could …
- I'd like to thank …
- My role model is …
- When I exercise I feel …
- When I'm angry I…
- I feel the most energized by…
- The best lesson I've learned so far is…
- I want to learn how to…

Buzzword: Mental Health

The best gift I have ever given myself was gathering up the courage to go to therapy. I'm so grateful that the stigma around mental health is going down. Thirty years ago, one would have to be in full-blown crisis mode before seeking therapy. If people would've known about it, they would've called you crazy and treated you like you were contagious.

I dream of the day when we see mental health as important as our physical health. Just like we check in with our primary care physicians and have our bodies checked and blood work done annually, it would be great if we had a mental health professional we check in with a few times a year at the very least, and more when we need it. Someone to help us pause, reflect, and process the events and relationships in our lives.

Mental health is how we think, feel, and act. When this is out of balance, we need to have tools to help ourselves get back in balance. Sometimes, there are things we can do on our own or learn how to do on our own. Sometimes it takes more, like therapy or medication.

Here's the thing: finding a therapist can sometimes feel like buying a new pair of jeans. You know what you want, but sometimes you have to try on a few pairs until you find one that vibes with you. My first therapist in New York didn't seem to hear me, gave me nothing to work on, and I felt like I was wasting my time. It took me fifteen years to officially get back into the therapy game after that. I had always known the importance of therapy and suggested it often to others. In moments of personal crisis, I reached out to the school counselors where I teach and found a badass life coach for a bit.

After a few years, I recognized that with each ending of the school year, my anxiety and my panic attacks were coming more often than they had in the year prior. One summer, while I was feeling good, I recognized that I didn't have the tools to deal with the upcoming pressures of school, parenting, and all the things that life throws at me. I acknowledged that my anxiety had been on the rise and that panic attacks were happening more often during the school year. I called a friend, who is a therapist, and asked her for a recommendation. I knew I needed help to manage my feelings and life while I felt stable—before I went into panic mode again. I'm glad I listened to my body and what I needed. Today, I see my rockstar therapist every two weeks. I am so grateful.

She helps me sift through all the thoughts rushing through my head. She helps me dig deeper into my true feelings instead of burying them. (Did you know you can bury things for DECADES?! And they subconsciously can haunt you?! It's true.) Mostly I feel like I am developing the tools to be able to be my best self in the wild world we live in. She has helped me learn to say no. She has helped me to be more present on a regular basis. She is a grounding force when I feel less-than. She has taught me to be mindful of where my energy goes. She's helping me take care of myself.

Bottom line: we all need therapy. Let's talk about it in a shame-free way. Stomp out stigma.

Until then, try these things:

- Exercise.
- Eating healthy.
- Social/group activities.
- Managing stress.
- Communicating your needs and feelings.
- Read books and take online classes about personal growth (like this one!).
- Seek out a professional. (How? Ask friends who they see. Look up therapists in your area online. Ask your doctor or school counselor for a recommendation.)

Mindful Self-Compassion

Mindfulness is a big buzzword these days. And rightfully so; it's useful and there is a lot of science backing it up. So, what does it mean? Basically, if we are being mindful it means we are being present and aware of our body's reactions physically and emotionally to the world around us and noticing these reactions without judgment . When we pause like this, we can make smarter and more rational decisions. When we do this we are actually training our brains to rewire and become more positive in our outlook.

Being aware of our reactions without judgment can be hard. Like, how many times have you (and I for that matter) made a mistake or fumbled and called yourself a name like "dumb" or "clumsy?" We tend to be the hardest on ourselves. Stuff we say about ourselves we never in a hundred years would say to a loved one. How do we change this? Well, we need to be more compassionate to OURSELVES. We need to love ourselves more and judge ourselves less. And it takes some tools and some practice.

Self-compassion is different from self-esteem, too. Self-esteem is great and easier when things are going well, but much harder when things aren't all rainbows and sunshine. Our brains are wired to remember the bad stuff; it kept us alive when we were cavemen and had to remember which berries were making us sick. It can help remind us that fire is hot and of the warning signs of predators. So, when things are bad or when bad things happen, it's a little harder to muster up big self-esteem. Self-compassion though, that is something we can work with always. Like loving yourself through the good times and the bad.

Self-compassion can be in our awareness (by being mindful) and is important at all times. But being kind to ourselves requires work. This is something we haven't been taught well and, friends, we need these tools. We need to practice. So, how do we do this? Glad you asked. Here are some of my favs.

- You catch yourself beating yourself up about something. What would you tell your best friend in this situation? Think about the actual script you would tell her/him. Now, say it to yourself. Use your name and everything. It might feel hokey, but it will work and will get easier with practice.

- Give yourself permission to be human. That's right. You do not need to do it all. And what you choose to do does not need to be perfect. Progress over perfection. Remind yourself every time you start beating yourself up for not being enough. You're totally enough.

- Practice some guided mindfulness. There are great apps out there to help you with this. I like Headspace, Breathe and Calm. Also, breathing deeply with your hands on your heart and repeating a positive affirmation can stimulate the good oxytocin in your brain.

- Finding time to practice gratitude for who we are and for the things we are thankful for. I find that when I'm super stressed and can't shut my mind off, doing this simple thing helps me to start shifting my mindset. It's even helpful to write it on paper. There is something that happens when you physically take pen to paper that helps your brain rewire in a positive, stress-reducing way.

- Seek professional help. If you are feeling like you have been in a dark funk for more than a couple of weeks and you can't get out of it, seek professionals. We go to the doctor for sprained ankles and strep throat, and sometimes, we need to seek tools from professionals to help our brains, too. And a simple search on the internet for your area will pull up a lot of resources, too.

Practicing self-compassion takes PRACTICE. You have to keep coming back to it, working on it. It's easy to fall into the negativity trap, but once you start being kind to yourself, you won't want to go back to anything else. You'll feel better about yourself and this is the best gift you could give yourself.

Would You Say That to a Friend?

Have you ever felt like you could find a hundred wonderful things to say about your friends but not even five about yourself? I'll bet that if you asked people that question you would find the same results. And this, my friends, needs to change. All of that crappy, judgmental, perfectionist, self-talk needs to stop. You would speak words of love and encouragement to a friend, and you need to treat yourself with the same grace and love.

Why is this a thing? We could look to a lot of different places for this answer. Maybe it was how we were raised. Maybe it's what we heard the adults saying when we were young and so now we do the same. Maybe it's the constant bombardment of beautiful people on the television and online that have been so airbrushed for so much of our lives. Maybe we don't even realize that what they look like is brought to us by "smoke and mirrors" and not reality. Maybe we've been picked on or hurt so much that we're starting to believe all of the negative lies that are thrown at us.

Whatever the reason, we need to take it upon ourselves to do better and change this, and it starts with you. It starts with how you talk about yourself. Do you say things like, "I'm so dumb," "I'm so ugly," or "I'll never find love?" Do you constantly compare yourself to everyone else who seems to be more put together, polished, and funny? (Spoiler: nobody has it all together, but some people are really skilled at pretending that they do.)

How do you talk about the people around you? Are you always criticizing the people around you? If you're constantly judging the people around you and constantly judging yourself, you'll never feel good. Cut yourself some slack. Be kind to yourself and others.

Now, I'm not telling you to tell yourself that you are perfect and can do no wrong. Because that's not true either. Everybody is human, everybody makes mistakes, and nobody is perfect, but, we are a work in progress. Progress over perfection. In the immortal words of Maya Angelou, when you know better, you do better.

If you can own up to your mistakes, learn from them, move on and do better next time, you will be much happier, and when you do something that makes you feel good or is a success in your world, celebrate it! Did you do well on a test? Did you do something creative? Have you been working your butt off to be healthy? Did you give of your time to someone that needed it? That's awesome. Celebrate yourself! Take the time to congratulate yourself. Remember all of the positives.

The next time you look in the mirror, and you think to yourself, "I'm not enough..."

JUST STOP.

YOU ARE ENOUGH.

You have hands that lift and help. You have legs that run and jump and leap. You have eyes that see beauty in the world. You have a mouth that smiles, and when it does, it lights up a room. You have a talent; it might be different than the people around you but it's there. You have a heart that beats strongly. You have a spirit that wants to do good and be good. You can see the good in your friends, but you also need to see it in yourself.

Try this: I would like to encourage you to take out a notebook or journal or even a scrap piece of paper. I want you to write down ten things that you like about yourself that have nothing to do with anything that you've purchased. (Do not tell yourself that you like yourself because you have a fabulous shoe collection. Think about who you are and what you have done.) And be patient if this takes you a while. Keep working at it.

We are all a work in progress, and you are enough.

Stop SHOULDING on Yourself

I think a lot of us feel like we are constantly in a state of competition—with each other and with ourselves. Whether you're comparing your outfit or your grades to a girl in school, or you're comparing your vacation to another's, or your body to everyone else's on Instagram, we have all felt this nagging feeling within ourselves at some point. I know I'm not alone here.

So, in the quest for seeing our own worth and value, I offer this:

You can achieve so much, but you don't have to do it all.

Especially ALL AT ONCE.

If you're like me, you might actually have to repeat this like a mantra sometimes.

Sometimes, we think we SHOULD do certain things all of the time. When we don't complete all of the tasks we put pressure on ourselves to do, we end up feeling inadequate. Well, here's the thing... SHOULD is a shaming word. Think about it.

I should lose weight.

I should make a homemade gift.

I should call more often.

I should go to the gym.

I should stay later at work.

I should take the kids on an outing.

I should....

The. List. Never. Stops.

Yes, some of these things are important and healthy, but, you can't do all of them, all of the time. Prioritize, make a plan, and take some of the things OFF of your list, until a later time when you can give them your attention. Communicate with the people in your world. If you have a choir concert on the same night you have two tests to prep for, it's okay to tell your group that you won't be able to make cookies for the lunch party the following day. People will have grace with you. And if they don't, that's their business. You were protecting your energy and taking care of yourself. No shame in that.

It's okay to let some of your "shoulds" go. If they're important, schedule them in. If they're not at the top of your list, get to them later. And sometimes, it's okay to let them—and the guilt—go.

You are enough and as a wise woman once told me, STOP SHOULDING ON YOURSELF.

PART 2:

Relationships with Others

Dear You,

I see you over there. Smart, beautiful, and in such a knot on the inside trying to be the perfect person to everyone you come across. Please take a deep breath and be still. You are enough. Your hard work doesn't need to be perfect. You don't need to be perfect. Nobody expects you to be. (And if they do, then maybe those aren't your people.)

Love, LP

P.S. Your mantra.. I am enough. xo

Rings of Trust

Relationships can be tricky because humans are so complicated. We carry a lot of things around in our heads and in our histories. Start first by assessing how you feel in different relationships. How does your body feel when you are around someone? Do you feel like you're walking on eggshells? Do they make you want to be the best version of you? How are you connecting with each other?

When thinking about all of the relationships you have in your life, it's sometimes helpful to think in terms of categories as well. I like to visualize this as "rings of trust." Basically, this is a way for us to evaluate an inner circle of friends versus an outer circle of acquaintances. Envision the rings on a tree; you are in the center. The people you trust the most, the people you'd call in a crisis or when you win the lotto, or when you're hurting, are in the rings closest to you. The further out you go are the people you know, but wouldn't necessarily confide your secrets to. Even further out are acquaintances. Furthest out are strangers and social media. Think in terms of all relationships, too, not just the people you see daily. Think about extended family, neighbors, teammates, etc.

One of the things people often struggle with is assuming everyone who is a "friend" or "follower" in the realms of social media, is a real friend in real life. Not the case. You do not need to share every bit of your life online. You do not need to put all of your medical details or every time your kid takes a BM out there for the world. You do not need to post a story every time you go shopping. And you also don't need to air your dirty laundry or anyone else's. Remember, if it's not your story to tell, don't tell it. This doesn't mean I don't want you to use your voice; quite the opposite. Your voice matters, but make sure that what you put out in the world is true and helpful. (IG images of wine and cheese included.)

In high school, my best friend, Michele, had a crush on a nice football player named Kevin. At some point, for reasons I don't even know or understand twenty years later, I told him she didn't just like him, but she like-liked him. She found out quickly and I felt awful, and she was rightfully mad. And, if she had been keeping a ring of trust diagram, I would have been knocked a few rings out. So, how did I get back into her circle? I had to do a few things.

I had to apologize and feel sincere about it; face to face. I had to recognize my mistake and try to make it right.

I had to start being trustworthy again; over and over. To my memory, I never violated her trust like that again. But it did take time to earn it back. When you've made a mistake, even if you're sincere in your apology and feel a lot of remorse, the hurt is still there. Hopefully, time will heal it, but you also need to be patient.

And what if someone has violated your trust? Well, you will need to decide if you can find it in your heart to let that person back in. That person will need to start earning your trust back. They will need to prove their trustworthiness. But, what if they continue to make choices that violate your trust or go against your moral compass or your sense of safety? What if their values don't line up with yours? Maybe it's time to start drifting apart. Maybe they moved to those outer levels on your rings of trust.

I tend to not make this a big production. I can mentally wish them well and move on. I do not need to be mean or rude. I just stop making plans with them, stop sending as many messages, and stop telling them my secrets. I find new friends. Good or bad, I choose to do this to protect my heart and my sense of safety. And if I'm being honest, I also tend to shy away from conflict unless it's absolutely necessary. A better, braver, and more honest action might be to have a real and upfront conversation with the toxic friend, and let the chips land where they land, and deal with the potential fallout.

I think most people find this challenging. We do not find joy in potentially hurting or disappointing others, and hard conversations are hard, but often the most important. But sometimes, we have to let go of people who are toxic. In doing so, we are loving and respecting ourselves.

So, what does toxic looks like? Here is a checklist describing love and toxicity.

Love:

- treats you with respect
- never puts you down
- listens to your ideas
- compromises
- is proud of your successes
- is caring and honest
- shares some of your interests
- is positive
- respects your family and friends
- is understanding
- doesn't pressure you

NOT Love:

- disregards your boundaries
- makes fun of the things you like
- doesn't listen to you
- is aggressively stubborn
- doesn't tell their friends about you
- lies to you
- physically or emotionally hurts you
- is extremely negative, all the time
- does not care about your personal life
- is not supportive
- threatens you

Take some time with this, reflecting on specific relationships in your life. It's also a great tool when you do start to have doubts in a relationship because you can compare the actions on the list to the ones happening to you.

You deserve the love side but you have to set the boundaries for it. If you don't love yourself enough to do that, people will continue to walk all over you, disrespect you and bring you down. You deserve the people who will support and nurture you, and when you start evaluating your rings of trust and setting boundaries both for yourself and for others, you will find that as you purge toxic patterns from your life, you become happier and mentally healthier.

How to Listen

From an early age, we hear, "listen carefully" from the adults in our world. Caregivers want to keep us safe. Teachers want to help us learn by giving examples and directions. Parents want us to do our list of chores. (Those scattered socks around the house are not going to pick themselves up!) We are taught to hear and act. Hear and react. Repeat. But we are not always really listening. What does it mean to really listen? What does it look like to listen and not react immediately?

It seems like these days we often hear people just enough to respond quickly. We want to agree or to commiserate. We want to argue or put someone in their place. Sometimes, we just want to fix someone's problem because we think we're helping. And unfortunately, we are staring at a screen while someone in front of us is telling us their story. The problem here is that we're not fully present with the person speaking. We're trying to quickly solve something or pretending to be a good listener by catching most of what we hear. But we're not really listening.

For example, your friend has just gotten some bad news from his mom. He starts to tell you his story while you are scrolling your IG feed. You give him a well-timed "oh no" and "I'm so sorry." Then you pause scrolling to one-up his story with one of your own before he's even done processing his bad news. Then, you offer him some candy to take his mind off of it. You didn't really help at all.

Or what if your friend was explaining how so-and-so was acting like an asshole on the way to school? And before she's even done talking, you're on your way to confront the fool and make a scene like a lunatic. She didn't need you to do that and she didn't ask you to do that. Your reaction is making the situation worse for everyone.

In both of these scenarios, you are not being a very good listener. You're not being present. You're not taking into account what your friend really needs. You are quickly reacting without much thought. They need a sounding board to process their thoughts. It's fine to want to help, but AFTER you've gotten the whole story and AFTER they've said all they need to say. And AFTER you have asked what kind of support they'd like. Do they just want to vent? Do they want your opinion? Ask. And really listen.

So, what does a good listener look like?

Actively engaged.

Here's how:

1. Put your phone face down or away.

2. Turn your body toward the speaker.

3. Make eye contact.

4. Try not to interrupt.

5. Ask questions about the story to get clarity without judgment .

6. Ask how your friend FEELS.

7. Ask your friend what they want and need from you.

8. Ask if they'd like to brainstorm solutions or scenarios.

9. Ask if they just need to "get it out" and vent without you trying to fix anything.

10. When your time is through, do not tell the story to others. It's not your story to tell. This is gossip and leads to mistrust.

When people are talking, they want to feel heard. They want to feel seen and understood. Often, they just need to get something off their mind and into the open. It's not your job to compete with their story or to fix what is perceived to be wrong. As a friend, it's your job to be present and engaged. You can encourage bravery and respect vulnerability. You can encourage someone to seek professional help (like a therapist, doctor, or law enforcement) if they need it.

The Power of the Pause

When I was younger, I did a lot of reacting to things, which didn't always lead to optimal results; it usually involved snap judgments and loud outbursts. I also spent a lot of time reacting to myself and my body in unhealthy ways. I tried yo-yo fad diets, I was judgmental toward people around me, I spent money I didn't actually have, and I yelled when I was frustrated. Holy shit, so much yelling. (Sorry, my boys. You'll talk to your therapist, I'm sure.) Sometimes I was able to make and follow through with goals but never understood the why behind them.

Sometimes, my achievements weren't things I actually wanted to do, but things that I thought I should do. (There's that shaming word again.) It took me a long time to realize that stopping, pausing, and reflecting helped project me closer to where I really wanted to be, and recognize when I was sabotaging myself.

The "stop-pause-reflect" helps me on a daily basis. In the moment, the power of the pause is literally you telling yourself to stop. Breathe. Think. What's happening right now? How are you feeling? What are the facts? (Feelings aren't facts.) What is the next right thing to do? How do you want to feel? How can you make that happen?

If I remember to do this (and I do need frequent self-check-ins), I am less yell-y with my kids, more likely to say no to tasks that aren't my responsibility and make better and more thoughtful decisions. It gives me time to think. A few seconds might be all I need, and if I need more time to make a decision, the pause allows me to see that and respond accordingly with a, "I'll get back to you on that."

Pausing tells your brain that there's no immediate danger. Pausing reminds you that you always have a choice in how you react. Pausing allows you to check in with your feelings quickly. Pausing reminds you that your attitude makes a world of difference.

Now, I try to stop, pause, and think before reacting and making rash decisions. The power of the pause can also be a bigger, more planned event. For me, it starts with a new year. Or a new season, depending on my mood. I learned this practice at a conference a few years back and it is pure magic. It looks a little like this:

- First, block out a few hours for yourself. Alone. Leave the house, lock yourself in your closet, wherever you can be alone. And tell the people in your house that you are having a date with yourself.

- Find your journal, or find a lovely new shiny one. I start by writing down a series of questions first, leaving a blank page underneath each one. I don't answer them immediately. Use these to start and add your own, too.

Look back to move forward questions:

- What are you proud of?
- What have your patterns been? (Work, home, relationships)
- What has been useful? What has not been useful?
- What would you like to do better? What themes do you notice from this brainstorm?

Move-ahead questions:

- What do you want to accomplish? (This year? This month? Or this quarter?)
- Reread what you have written. What words jump out at you?

What are your intentions for the new year (or next month, etc.) in these four categories?

- Personal growth.
- Patterns/practices.
- Relationships.
- Work/location/school.

What three priorities can you create from these intentions? Once the three priorities have been established, I write them pretty and hang them up. Everyone needs a personal reminder.

I love this practice so much. It reminds me of the good work I've done and allows me to dream of what comes next! This might seem silly or unimportant to some, but it's quite the opposite. Too often we just keep plugging ahead because life keeps moving and things get thrown at us. Sometimes life makes you feel like a hamster on a wheel to nowhere. But it's not. You are doing great things! You deserve to give yourself some accolades. Even for the little things.

Looking back also helps us to identify our bad habits and patterns. Without looking at our weaknesses, we can't grow stronger. We can't grow into the best versions of ourselves. And we deserve to be the best, happiest versions of ourselves that we can be.

So, whether we're thinking long-term or short-term, pausing is the magic we give ourselves to do and be our best. We don't want to live out of the fear-based reactionary response part of our brains unless we're being chased by a wild animal or a serial killer. We want to make decisions with intention and purpose as much as possible. The power of the pause will get us there.

Revelation

I had a revelation recently. My brother and sister-in-law throw these amazing parties. This one was for the kids and involved renting a foam machine. (Think: constant stream of giant bubbles.) I was the only adult that got into it. I had planned on going in, because when I heard about it I thought, 'Why not? You only live once. Why not take an opportunity to do something new.' But no other adults were going in. Everybody's perfectly curled locks would get ruined, so I understand. I stood around making bubble crowns with my youngest and my niece and even some other littles that I didn't know. And when I got out and was changing out of my wet muddy soapy clothes, I wondered why I even bothered. Sure, it was fun but not life-changing fun or even something that had ever been on my bucket list, and now, I had weird soapy greasy looking hair. But I kept coming back to the old cliche: You only live once. I kept thinking that if tomorrow was my last day on earth I would've wanted to have gone into the foam. And honestly, if I really dive into my psyche, the passing of my college roommate this summer has really got me thinking more about how I spend my time. I want to make a real conscious effort not to waste opportunities when they present themselves. This was one of those moments.

A part of me was saying, "You should clean the house; you should finish grading those papers; you should work on your book." (Remember that chapter on should is a shaming word?! See? Right there.) But a foam pit with kids seems like an opportunity that one should not miss.

When I think back to the adults in my life when I was younger, some of them really engaged with me and played. That meant so much to me. I want to be that example. Sometimes I need a break and I do just want to sit on the sidelines, and that's totally okay. But when I'm able, I do want to be active, and I do want to participate, and I do want to be a good example. I want to model this behavior because it's important.

Saying yes to fun can build relationships and MAKE YOU FEEL ALIVE. Doing something new makes you feel a little more whole. Breaking up the daily tasks and the repetitive motions in life is energizing and eye-opening.

If It's Not Your Story, Don't Tell It

I was not always my best self when I was a teenager. I thoroughly enjoyed hearing gossip about people and then finding someone else to tell the story to. I admit now that I am very ashamed of this behavior. I'm embarrassed that I'm writing that and admitting it out loud. But I'm trying to give some grace to my younger self whose prefrontal cortex hadn't fully developed yet. Nobody is perfect.

Looking back, I think I may have been deflecting my own insecurities by gossiping. I think my sixteen-year-old self subconsciously thought that if I talked about somebody else's (sometimes fictional) drama then people would be focused on that, and not on me and my own shortcomings. And honestly, as a child hearing adults talking about other adults in a gossipy way was normal for me. Now, as a grown-up I'm very aware of this behavior and I try not to engage in it. Especially with my students and my children.

Here's the thing: Telling someone else's story does you no good. First, it shows people that you can't be trusted. Spreading stories—lies or not—also does something to your spirit. It somehow tarnishes your light when you tell someone else's story. Your light, the essence of who you are shrinks when you (inadvertently or not) try to dim someone else's.

Something I share with my students and my children is, "if it's not your story, don't share it." This is an important statement and keeps everything in check. And consider that EVERYONE has a story and what you think you know might not be reality or the full truth. Start getting into the habit of asking yourself the question: Is this my story to tell? Only tell it if the answer is "yes" AND you want to share it.

Words matter. Your story is important. Sharing it can help you grow and heal. Sharing your own story brings out your voice, making others feel less alone. But that's YOUR story. You have the choice and the power here. Do not share someone else's. When you do that, you are taking away their voice, their choice, and their power.

One of the hardest things to do is to speak up or say "not my story" when your friends are pressuring you for information. I think the easiest thing to do is to say, "not my story to tell, you'll need to ask him/her." Or if you have only heard something second-hand, say nothing. It's not your tale to tell.

Now, the only exception to this is if you suspect someone is going to harm themselves or others. ALWAYS seek help in these cases. Find a trusted adult or professional in these cases. This person will know the best next steps, and if they don't, they'll have the knowledge and resources to move in the right direction.

We always want to do things to make us feel better and deflect people from seeing the parts of us that are less than desirable. It's human nature BUT it can be checked when we are self-aware. Be aware when conversation turns to gossip and when you're spreading lies or stories that don't belong to you. If it's your habit to engage in gossip, people will start to lose trust in you. It's hard to have friends and to be a friend if you can't be trusted. If your conversations are always about others in a negative way, it's time for a new conversation. If someone told you something in confidence and you tell someone else, you are just proving how untrustworthy you are to both parties.

If you are sharing how you were treated by someone and having a conversation around behavior, that discussion can actually benefit you and your friend group. Talking about behavior (not people) can help you work out proper social or antisocial behavior. This is different from gossiping because you're telling your own story.

Remember, checking yourself and becoming self-aware will help you stay true to yourself. It will show others that you can be trusted. It will help you grow into the best possible version of yourself.

When to Screw Politeness

I was taught, like so many other women, some strange rules growing up about manners that only seemed to apply to my female gender specifically. Whether this was from society at the time or how we were raised in our families can be debated, but either way, I know I'm not alone, and I see it in my own students, too. The need to please others to make THEM feel more at ease often comes before our own needs of self-preservation. These were all subliminal learnings: No one sat me down and told me these things.

Here are some things I had to UNLEARN to become a strong, whole human:

- Don't rock the boat.

- Laugh at his jokes, even if they're racist or sexist. If you don't, people will think you're rude or lack a sense of humor.

- If you respond forcefully to sexual advances in a negative way you'll be considered a prude or a bitch. On the flip side, if you respond too eagerly, you're a slut. So, good luck walking that tightrope.

- It's more important to accommodate others' needs than your own, so you're not perceived as rude or heartless. Basically, don't have boundaries. If someone needs something, bend over backward to make it happen because that's what "good girls" do.

- Give up your time and energy "because they're family" even if they're rude, ungrateful and using you without giving you the same courtesy.

- Be gracious when someone pressures you and makes you feel uncomfortable with unwanted attention.

- Being pretty is more important than being smart.

- Even if you're smarter or know more about a topic, downplay your intellect to keep his ego from getting bruised.

Unlearning things like this takes WORK. First of all, I didn't even realize I was doing most of these things until my husband started questioning me when we were first married. Sometimes I would look to him for permission or approval to gauge if I should do something or not. I felt like I had to make sure his needs were completely met before I even thought about mine. He started calling me out on this. These patterns had been ingrained in me for so long, I only recognized that I didn't like how I felt after he pointed out these people-pleasing patterns. In these moments, I didn't like myself, found myself weak, and would often beat myself up after the fact. It was hard to see my own patterns early on, but I could see them in other women. I would silently judge other women, but I didn't have the guts or the self-realization to look at myself until much later.

When I became a mother, I learned very quickly that my baby was much happier when we kept a consistent schedule. This schedule of mealtimes, nap times, and bedtimes was not to be broken unless there was an emergency. When we did break our routine, he turned into a monster, and we were all miserable. I remember very clearly that certain family members really tried to shame me into keeping him up late. They would try to guilt me into keeping him up late so I could still celebrate with the group. They would try to feed him things that weren't part of his diet behind my back, and I was the one that felt bad! This is when I realized that my need to please was overpowering my needs and the needs of my baby. This is one of the first times I remember sticking up for myself to the elders in my family. And after the initial uncomfortable feeling of not making everyone happy, I actually felt proud of myself. Confident, and dare I say, happy? After this, it got easier to speak up for myself.

Last winter my neighbor was going through one of those break-ups where it didn't quite stick the first time. You know what I'm talking about. They break up, then they're back together a week later, then they're broken up again. But I knew this guy was a manipulating control freak with more baggage than an airport. No one but a therapist should make plans with him, but I digress. He was making my friend second-guess her parenting, tried to move in after a month of dating, threatened her, and tried to isolate her by turning her against her family. Textbook narcissist. After one of their break-ups, his car was parked in her driveway while our kids were playing outside. I asked her daughter if the man had been invited over. She replied, "Well, he asked if he could come over and my mom didn't want to be rude." Inside I was livid. I watched as my friend tried to ignore him and kept mowing her lawn. Then the man walked into her house like he lived there. I was scared for her safety. I was worried that she was so concerned about being polite to this man that she was putting herself and her child in danger.

Friends, this is a case of screw-politeness.

Just because someone wants something from you doesn't mean you have to give it. Whether it's your time, to sit in your space, your sexual attention, your approval, etc. If you do not want to do something, it is not rude to voice your opinion. It is not rude to say, "no," "no thanks," or "not today." If someone is disappointed in your response, it's okay. You can't make people happy every second of every day. You will lose yourself, and this is not your job. We are only responsible for our own happiness and attitude toward life.

Your voice and your opinion matter. Setting boundaries is important to your mental health and overall well-being. This doesn't mean you have to be rude, but it will take some calm assertiveness and a firm tone.

Here are some examples:

Person: What are you doing? Can I come over?
You: I'm busy, not today. (Or a simple, no thanks.)

Person: Want to hang out?
You: No thanks, not today.

Person: I bought you dinner, you owe me a (insert sexual act).
You: No (Seriously, only do things with your body if YOU also desire it. And seriously, that "give me sexual favors in return for normal human decency" is a douchebag thing to do. Sexual behavior is a CONSENTING two-way street.)

Person: We need you at our meeting at six PM on Friday. (On a Wednesday when you have tickets to a concert on Friday night. Or, even if you don't have Friday night plans. It's Friday night! You work hard all week.)
You: I am unavailable, but I'd be happy to give you my notes before I leave for the day. Thanks for understanding.

Please note a couple of things in my quick scenarios. The responses are short, to the point and not wishy-washy, and there is no apology. You do not have to apologize when there is nothing to apologize for. Your needs and your wants are valid.

Your feelings do not need to be apologized for. You have done nothing wrong. You should apologize when you have hurt someone, made a mistake or spilled wine on the floor. You don't apologize for not wanting to hang out or for being unavailable. Saying you're sorry somehow implies that your actions are wrong. This is not true when your feelings and sometimes safety are on the line. Thank people for understanding your decision. Only apologize if you've made a mistake.

Sometimes we need to use our voice to say "no" when we're feeling other kinds of pressure. Pressure to dress or act a certain way, to drink or do drugs at a party, to engage in a political debate when we're not in the mood. I have always found this list from "Know Your Nos" from The Right to Resist very helpful when talking about HOW to stand up for yourself.

Avoiding/Evasive NO... "Hey, did you see what they just did?"

Avoiding means:

- Changing the subject.

- Staying away from the issue.

- Trying to distract the person putting on the pressure.

Passive NO... "Um, sorry, I can't, I have a ...thing..."

Being passive means:

- Saying not weakly.

- Mumbling.

- Making up lame excuses.

- Acting wimpy.

Aggressive NO... "No way, stupid. That's for losers."

Being aggressive means:

- Pushing people around.

- Threatening or blaming them.

- Putting them down.

- Acting angry.

Know-It-All NO... "No and you shouldn't either. It's really bad for you."

Being a know-it-all means:

- Giving lots of facts, real or fake.

- Acting superior.

- Acting judgmental

- Telling others how they are feeling

<u>Assertive NO... "No, thanks."</u>

- Eye Contact

- Keep it simple

- Walk away

This last one, the Assertive NO, is the best. It is the most concrete and straight forward.

Sometimes it's helpful to role-play possible scenarios out loud. When we do this we get used to saying the words we need to use, and it becomes more natural to speak our truth when the words flow easier. Try it in front of a mirror sometimes. It will feel awkward at first, but with practice, it'll be much easier to speak the words in the real world.

Boundaries for Our Well-Being

We talk a lot about physical boundaries as we are growing up. We are taught where people can and can't put their hands. Don't hit! Don't touch! We even set boundaries on our language. You probably talk to your friends in a different way than you talk to your teachers or your boss. Unfortunately, we don't always teach great boundary skills with our time or our energy. This is something I started learning in my thirties and still have to work on today. I was taught all the skills to be ambitious and successful, but I was never taught to protect my energy and time, or to make time for joy.

The first thing I learned about time boundaries was that I needed to be okay with saying "no." I started by saying no to volunteer opportunities that I didn't have time for and that didn't serve me or my family. That might sound selfish to some, but trust me, I still volunteer my time and give back. I'm just not on every. single. committee. Just because I am capable of doing something, doesn't mean I have to do it; I had to get rid of the "should" mentality, the shaming word. It can make you feel bad for not doing something. I also had to realize that there were other people that could step up and pitch in. I didn't always have to say yes.

When my kids were in elementary school I would frequently get emails to sign up for volunteer things—especially the holiday parties. I would sign up for anything that I could. I would make a fruit bowl, turn cheese sticks into ghosts, find the correct table-cloths, and sign up to do cleanup. This went on for years until I realized I didn't need to do all of this. Who was I trying to impress? No one. Or maybe myself? Or the other moms? I think I wanted to prove to myself and everyone else that I really could "do it all." I still sign up for some things but not everything, and not every time.

I am a people pleaser. I was trying not to let anyone down. When I realized I could just sign up for the paper products and/or cleanup duty, I felt a huge weight lifted off my shoulders. Writing this now I feel a little silly. You might be thinking, "no crap, lady, nobody said you have to do it all." But, here's the thing: somehow it got into my head that I had to do it all, all the time. It is exhausting, and I know that I am not alone. So many of my friends fall into this trap all the time.

So, fast forward a decade, and setting boundaries with acquaintances is easy for me. I've never gotten backlash. And if I did and it was behind my back, that's their business. It is harder to set up boundaries with family and friends. You love these people. You would probably, literally, give them the shirt off your back if they needed it. But, sometimes, it's just too much.

When we lived in New York and most of my family was in Michigan, we would buy a Christmas gift for every person in the extended family. Every. Single. Person. And then ship all of these gifts back to Michigan. Aunts, uncles, cousins, cousins' babies, their new spouses, siblings, and grandparents. EVERYONE. We could not afford this, and we didn't enjoy it. I orchestrated the shopping, the wrapping, and the shipping. My husband stressed about the money; we were racking up more credit card debt. Why? Because that's the way it had always been in my family. It was expected. If I didn't do it, I thought people would be mad, they would gossip about it, and they wouldn't like me anymore. After a couple of years of this stress and an ever-growing family, it was decided as a collective group that we would just buy for the kids, not the adults. Some people didn't like this, but mostly it seemed like a good idea. But, as more babies were born into the family and people were all spread out, it felt like a laborious chore again. We weren't a super tight knit group and our gifts were like a check-the-box not, an I-know-you'll-love-this. Finally, in an act of bravery, my cousin, Stefani, respectfully bowed out of all extended family gift-giving. Were some people disappointed? Maybe. Were people mad? Not to my knowledge. I was relieved. I thought she was smart and I followed suit in my own way. I could focus my time and money on my own kids and the people in my life that I'm close with. Stef was able to set up a boundary for herself and her family that fit with her values, and in this case, her budget, too.

Sometimes we do need to step up and help out when it's uncomfortable or inconvenient. Sometimes, emergencies happen. This is being a good human. After my grandmother passed, my grandfather was alone and had to learn how to do things more independently. I can't imagine the grief and the heartache that came with that time in his life. Everyone rallied around him to help out but, many years later, some people set up boundaries with their time and labor. He kept asking people to do things he was capable of doing on his own but didn't want to do because my grandmother had always done them for him. The people that didn't set boundaries were run ragged and resented the ones that did set boundaries. Giving too much of your time and energy to people who are competent and capable on their own might put your health and well-being at risk.

What about the guilt of letting people down? I struggled with that in the past, and then I realized that if they can't understand that I need to take care of myself and my family as a priority, and if they can't understand boundaries, that is their problem. People not understanding why I set boundaries are often the same people who lack boundaries themselves.

I've been getting better with boundaries, but it's still hard. I don't enjoy disappointing people. I'm still working on letting go of guilt. But here's the thing: rational people might be bummed, but they will also understand. They understand that although you might look like a superhero on social media, you are just a mere mortal with time and money constraints. They will still love you.

My oldest friend, whom I love very much, got married in a private ceremony and scheduled her out-of-state reception for a few months later. We received a save-the-date card and everything. We couldn't all go as a family, so I booked a flight and rented a car for myself. Adventure awaits! A couple of months before the reception, she canceled it for valid reasons of her own. (She was setting her own boundaries. Yay!) She still extended an invitation to a few people to visit her during the planned reception time. And although the reception was canceled, she expressed wanting to feel special and celebrated so we started organizing dinners and showers for her. But, that wasn't what she needed either, so we listened to her and decided we were just going to show up and be ready for anything.

Two weeks before the trip, her plans changed again in a way that I couldn't make work. So, I had to make a hard phone call. I had to let her know that I was not going to be able to manage the new version of her celebratory weekend after all. I did not want to, but I needed to put myself first in this scenario.

As I write this first draft, it's the weekend I'm supposed to be flying out to celebrate my friend. I'm sad for my friend, and I do feel some guilt, but I'm not ashamed. I set a boundary for myself that was best for my well-being, our family's budget, and my precious time. She didn't say much when I reached out to her this week. I suspect she might feel hurt or mad, and I get it; I disappointed her. But she's also smart and rational; as of the publication of this book, all is well in our friendship.

Sometimes when you set boundaries, people are disappointed. It's okay; you might be disappointed sometimes, too. We all have a choice in our attitudes when we feel let down. We can let it turn into anger and let negative energy build up, making us miserable. Or we can choose compassion and understanding and move on. But, if we don't set these boundaries, we stretch ourselves too thin. We aren't able to take care of ourselves because we're taking care of everyone else. We lose ourselves when we try to please everyone else. We become resentful of people and tasks, and that feels miserable. It's not selfish to choose your well-being. Like the airplane with the oxygen masks, you must put yours on first before helping others. It's not just okay, it's necessary to sustain a whole, full life.

When I think about boundaries now, I visualize a cute little house with a yard and a white picket fence. I am the house, the yard is what I'm willing to do, and the fence is the boundaries in my life that I've set up. I get to decide who comes into the yard and what activities I let in or participate in. People too; some people get to come all the way in. Others I meet at the fence for a chat, but they don't come into the yard. If the request is going to make me feel like a locomotive is plowing through my yard/house visual, I give a polite, "Unfortunately, I can't make it. Thanks for understanding!" That is explanation enough.

How Do We Mend Fences?

As I write this chapter, we are in what feels like the longest presidential election week in history. It's November of 2020 and Joe Biden and Kamala Harris have won but it still very much feels like we are a nation divided, and this is breaking my heart. Growing up, I remember family members debating politics but never with the venom, disrespect, and hatred that I see now. Of course, there will be disappointment when your "team" loses. There is a normal period of mourning and discontent, anger, and frustration. I have felt this several times after a presidential election and, of course, at other times in life. But this time it feels different.

In the past, we were always able to see past political differences and still join each other at the table. And now we have villainized each other to the point that anything the other side says or does is wrong and evil. Any person on the other side is automatically our enemy. Families that used to enjoy each other's company have gotten so snarky, mean, and unmoving toward each other that they don't break bread together anymore. The sad reality is that they've forgotten compassion, empathy, and all of the commonalities we have. Our ideas on how to get there may be different, but our goals are generally similar. We want safety and security. We want to feel free to be who we were born to be.

I think the anger and separation that we feel are fear based. Fear of something being taken from us, fear of the unknown, fear for our lives and livelihoods, and sometimes fear of retaliation. Fear can rear its ugly head in a lot of ways, and when fear dominates the public stage of politics, it's hard not to feed into this fear and make it your own.

So, back to the original question… How do we mend fences and move forward in our personal lives?

Here are some thoughts:

- Set some ground rules at gatherings. Maybe actually avoiding talking about any divisive topic for a while at the table is a good idea.

- Assume positive intent. Imagine that a person is starting from a well-intended place and is doing their best.

- Find items and activities of common interest to share.

- Play games that bring back a feeling of nostalgia and warmth.

- Call someone you haven't talked to in a while and extend the olive branch and just talk about your personal lives.

- Make someone a cup of tea, that always helps me.

- Don't gloat.

- Remember this: all people want to feel heard and loved. Show them you see them and hear them. You don't have to agree but you can listen.

- Check yourself and your own bias. As humans, we have biases. But once we are aware and we can check them, we can acknowledge them and fix the ones that are wrong.

- Find neutral ground… A ball game, sharing a recipe, lending a book, bringing over baked goods, reminiscing over a family photo or heirloom.

- Explain your absence and how you've been feeling. Name it and claim it. Clear the air. Allow the others to do the same.

- Family therapy? If this is not a thing, maybe it should be.

- Set boundaries on what you will and won't get into conversations about.

Our country needs to mend its fences, and it needs to come back to humanity within its borders.

We Have More in Common with Each Other

Growing up we tend to pair up and group up with people who act like us, dress like us, etc. This is a very natural thing for us to do as humans, but it also really limits our experiences if we don't ever reach out. Yes, it's important to have a tribe and to love them hard, but it's equally important to learn from people outside of the bubble we tend to find comfort in. Every once in a while, attend an event outside of your racial, ethnic, or religious experience. Look for workshops or festivals in your area that you might find new and interesting.

When I went off to college, I met a girl my freshman year. Her name was Lisa and we both worked at the front desk of our all-girls dorm, aptly nicknamed The Virgin Vaults. She was a year ahead of me, a little rough around the edges, and engaged in some risky behaviors that I had only ever read about in cautionary tales or seen in after-school specials. She looked like a hardened rockstar next to my innocent girl-next-door vibe, and I was fascinated by her. If we had been in high school, my mother would have forbidden me from hanging out with her outside of school. As a mother now, I sort of get it.

These days, everybody and their grandmother has a tattoo. But when I met Lisa, only veterans or people with "alternative lifestyles" had them. One of her tattoos was one of the monsters from Where the Wild Things Are and she held my hand when I got my first regrettable tattoo. She told me tales of dropping acid and tripping hard, which scared me, so I never did it. (Sometimes having control issues works well for me.) On occasion, we shared swigs of cheap whiskey some upper-classmen bought for us. What I learned by spending time with Front Desk Lisa was that although we came from different families, regions, and experiences, we really wanted the same things in life. We wanted to be loved, to feel heard, to protect the people that couldn't protect themselves, and to do better for the earth. We were just going about it in different ways. We were able to look past our Pollyanna/Rockstar differences and learn from each other and even have a friendship for a little while. We were able to see a fellow human being instead of the "other" label that divided us. We found commonalities in our lives, shared magazine articles about saving the planet, and promoted safe sex by handing out condoms and pamphlets to the other residents from our front desk perch. We did not stay friends after that year, and it was probably because our priorities in life were different. But meeting Lisa showed me how to judge less and ask more questions.

My old high school friend, Chad, came out as a proud gay man when we were in college, and his story broke my heart. I was NOT heartbroken because he was gay, I was upset by how he had been treated growing up. It was the nineties and it was very rare (well in my small northern town, anyway) for people to be openly gay. When he told me about how scared he was, and how he had attempted suicide because he felt like people hated him for who he was, it rocked my world. I had been a part of those subtle jabs without knowing their impact. Using the word "gay" to insult someone or something. (Like, you have a test to study for? That's gay.) And then, worse yet, if someone thought you might be gay or just really wanted to socially ruin you, they would start calling you gay. You would've been ostracized, attacked, shunned, and would have basically had an even worse high school life. Friends would have left; people would have gossiped. So, when my talented, funny, charming friend told me he was gay and he had found a supportive group of friends in college, I was so happy for him and proud of him. He was the bravest person I knew at that moment, and I felt honored that he trusted me with his truth. I also realized a couple of things.

One, using the word "gay" as a derogatory term was going to end for me and the people in my circles. Words matter and this is a lesson I still continue to teach. Yes, I still have to have this conversation with some students twenty years later, but thankfully, not as often. Two, Chad and I had a lot in common. At that moment, I was in the midst of an eating disorder, and what I realized was that we both wanted to feel comfortable in our own skin, we wanted people to love and accept us as we were. And we were just starting to realize that our voices in this world matter. Living our truth also feels a lot better than living a lie. Although, it may feel vulnerable at first. It's worth bravely going forward with it.

I feel like sometimes, it's easier for people to give into their natural bias than to take the time to really listen to others. Generally, we want the same things like safety, love, freedom, and acceptance. Our journeys and methods to get these things are different and that's where we start to come undone as a society. That's when we start seeing people as "other" somehow they become the enemy we want to fight against.

I have a photograph in my house of a Sudanese mother holding her child's hand outside of her mud hut. The sky and homes are very muted, but the mother is wearing a stunning red wrap. When I first saw this picture I was drawn to her because she was me and I was her. I realize, by all outside appearances, we are completely different in looks and in lifestyle. But I can assume we wanted the same things in the moments we were in. We wanted to love and protect our children. Her image has continued to inspire me to connect with people and find common ground, no matter how different we might look or how different our backgrounds are.

Finding common ground in humanity and others doesn't mean you have to be best friends with everyone you meet. It's a way to be respectful and to learn from others. It helps build human connection, which we all need in order to thrive. It builds empathy, which our society sometimes seems to lack these days.

Want to find more commonalities with people you encounter? Start by asking them some questions.

- Where did you grow up?

- When was the last time you laughed?

- What is your favorite movie?

- What is your dream concert?

- If you could have brunch anywhere in the world, where would you go?

- What are you reading?

- What are you most proud of?

The point is to find commonalities. In my experience, even if people can't always relate to a specific experience, they can relate to feeling a certain way. We have all experienced joy, fear, boredom, and disappointment. If we can start connecting with people in a more genuine way, we are helping to knit our world back together one kind gesture at a time.

Scared of Heights/Do It Scared

The first time I ever did a high ropes course was almost twenty years ago. I was terrified. I think I might have cried, and when I completed it, I felt like I could do anything if I just took a big breath first. I remembered that "after" feeling of accomplishment very well.

I remembered those feelings of accomplishment one spring when I was planning a field trip for the Lotus Project, a female empowering organization. I'm always telling the girls, "You don't need to be perfect; you need to be brave." Or, "Take healthy risks!" And I thought a high ropes course would help us do both of these things. I had grand visions: We get there, put on our helmets and gear, and then get our empowerment on! It was going to be a great team building and bonding experience.

So, when I stood on that platform an old wave of fear washed over me. I wanted to leave. How did my memory only remember the good stuff?! As they were harnessing me into my safety gear I looked out onto the ropes course and I thought out loud, "Whose terrible idea was this? Oh yeah... mine." I was not leading by example at that moment.

I realized then, that as a leader, these ladies were going to follow my cue. If I freaked out or refused to go, which honestly crossed my mind, then they would do the same thing if they were scared. They would give up without even trying, like I had thought about doing. So, I did the only thing I could think of. I pretended not to be scared. I faked it.

There were moments on the ropes course when most of us were hesitant. A few times, frozen in fear, needing to be coaxed or encouraged. A couple of us had to reach for a hand. We watched each other succeed. We asked for help and advice. We encouraged each other. We took deep breaths, and we just did it, and we did it scared. And we conquered that course! We pushed ourselves further than we thought we could. And it felt AMAZING. Especially after we were done. Super awesomely amazing!

Not only did we feel good about ourselves, but we learned some life lessons.

- Sometimes when you're taking a healthy risk, you need to do it scared.

- We all learned we were more capable than we thought we were.

- Encouragement matters. Even from people you don't know well.

- Seeking advice and asking for help is a good life lesson.

- Doing something challenging makes us stronger and better people.

- Not trying something new because you think you will look stupid is not an excuse.

- Feelings aren't facts.

- Focusing on the outcome of something in a positive way makes doing it a whole lot easier. Focusing on the negative holds you back.

I hope that my girls will remember how they felt this day. I hope they remember how they were conquering warrior women. I hope they hold onto that and remember that they can do anything when it comes to healthy risks.

And sometimes in life, you have to jump in and do it scared.

An Argument in Support of Strangers

"Don't talk to strangers" was something plugged into my head as a child. "Don't befriend anybody because you could potentially get hurt," and I get it; to a point. Our parents wanted to keep us safe. There are indeed bad people out there. But I think that knowing boundaries and being assertive might protect us more. Somehow this hyper-vigilant don't-talk-to-strangers turned all people we didn't know into the bad guys. I'd like to argue that engaging with new people can actually help us. It has the possibility and potential to connect us to other people in the world. It can create a network of compassion. It can help us learn new skills and open doors to new opportunities.

Last summer, while traveling in France, I went into a small art gallery in the town of Châteaux D'Azay le Rideau in the Loire Valley. (This town looks like a movie set. The opening song from Beauty and the Beast popped into my head several times while I was there.) When I walked into the wall-to-wall watercolor gallery, I was also walking into the artist's studio. There was a wall of windows overlooking a small, yet glorious garden, a large easel with good lighting, brushes and paints scattered about, and a desk area for business transactions. Plus, all of the finished artwork displayed on the other three walls. It was a small, yet powerful and inspiring setup.

I desperately wanted to compliment this man's space, but I spoke such little French. I managed to smile and say, "bonjour, c'est belle" while gesturing to the room. And then I broke into a quick English gush of, "you-are-so-talented-this-is-so-beautiful-I-love-the-gardens-I'm-a-history-teacher-this-village-is-magical." Fortunately, in a thick French accent, this man thanked me in English for my compliment and we had a lovely conversation. I was able to tell him that I admired his watercolors and that I had started dabbling in them myself during the pandemic. He told me how people would sometimes wander into his private garden while he was drinking his morning coffee and he would have to explain that it was a private place, but he could appreciate how the beauty draws people in. I told him I was a history teacher and how much I appreciated the richness of the history in this area. He reminded me that it's not just his history or France's history, but it's all part of human history. It's the history of our ancestors that connects us to this place and other places. He reminded me that before my ancestors settled and immigrated to the United States, they were here. He worded this sentiment so well, and it made me really feel more connected to him personally and to all of the humans around me; travelers and natives alike.

I could've just walked into his shop and not said anything. I could've just picked up one of the prints and a couple of postcards and paid my bill and gone on my way. But in this situation, I needed to reach out and compliment this man, and I'm so glad I did. The few minutes that we had of conversation impacted me. It made me see things in a new way. It reminded me of the connected fiber of humanity.

I have always loved history and have been especially drawn to the art, the fashion, and the stories of the people living it. La Samaritaine department store opened in Paris in 1869. It has this amazing art nouveau architecture inside and out. It was first opened to cater to the middle class. It closed in 2005 and was closed on the first two visits that I made to Paris. But this third time, it had just reopened after its decade of renovations. It was a pleasant surprise for this Francophile. I was excited to see the architectural elements and I could totally envision what it was like to shop here during the Belle Époque era. When I walked in, I was instantly mesmerized by the decorative iron staircases, the mosaics on the floor, and the murals on the wall. I didn't know what to expect as far as product was concerned, but I knew I wanted to buy something French. Specifically, something to make me feel Parisian. Looking around, I quickly realized that everything in my line of vision was high-end luxury. It was beautiful and I definitely could not afford it. Trust me, if I could walk into a shop and buy a Louis Vuitton bag or a vintage Dior dress, I would. But alas, this is not my lifestyle. I very quickly decided that I needed to buy something that I could afford and so I went to the cosmetics floor. I decided a lipstick was in my budget. So, I made my way to the Chanel cosmetics counter. I decided to try to stumble my way through some French and get some help from the Chanel counter girl. Luckily, she spoke some English and was able to help me try out several lipsticks and find one that fit me. She made me feel very luxurious and fancy. Before I checked out, she asked me if I would be interested in some samples. Oui! Oui! S'il vous plaît! She hooked me up. She wrapped all of my things and tissue paper and put them in a Chanel bag, and I walked out of there feeling like a million euros.

Engaging with a stranger in this scenario not only boosted my mood but also reminded me that I'm not so different from the people who work or shop in La

Samaritaine. As I walked through the store feeling like a misfit, this woman helped me feel like I belonged. I could've just picked something from the display and gone on my merry way, but I decided to take a healthy risk.

Engaging with new people doesn't just benefit us, but it can benefit them as well. We have a lot to offer to the world, in ways we don't even know. Last week, when I was in my local coffee shop working on lesson plans, the large table opened up and as I went to move to it, someone beat me to it. She saw me and smiled and said that she just needed to be near a plug and that we could share the table. So, I unpacked my laptop and my notebooks and got to work. I was frequently interrupted by my middle school child and his friends, but in a good way. They just wanted to chat. I hoped that we were not interrupting my table mate. About an hour into my work, this stranger passed a note to me. She wrote that my son was sweet and that the kids brought back fond memories of her own when they were younger. After the kids left, I thanked her for her note and introduced myself. It turns out that Paula is in education, like me, and was looking for work in an elementary school setting. Her focus is on trauma. She is helping students but also helping teachers understand how to work with students who have been affected by different traumas in their lives. And it just so happens that this is one of my passions as well. I directed her to my school district's website to look for openings. There were several and she had her application in that afternoon. I emailed some of my contacts in the district to give them a heads-up that Paula was going to be sending her résumé out.

I could have sat at that table all afternoon, just being polite and courteous. I could've thanked her for her note and not engaged any further, but I didn't. We had such a great conversation about education and how to make it better, where money needs to funnel to, and how to give kids the tools to be their best selves, the tools that are needed to be good functioning humans before the academics can start, and how to help teachers. It was such a beautiful conversation. If these two strangers hadn't actively engaged with one another it would not have happened.

Sometimes, we don't have the energy to engage with people we don't know. But I would like to encourage you to, on occasion, bring up the energy and the bravery to talk to somebody new. Not all conversations are life-changing, but sometimes, they are, and that's how we connect better to humanity. It's another way that we help ourselves grow emotionally and build up our own confidence. And building up our own confidence will help us have better conversations with the people that we interact with on a daily basis. Confidence helps us set up the boundaries that we need in order to grow and thrive.

How to Talk to People

I once asked for feedback on topics for an upcoming workshop with a group of teens. I was expecting heavy topic suggestons, and I was a little surprised when they wanted to know how to talk to strangers. They felt well-versed in messaging via text, but when it came to speaking out loud on the phone or face-to-face, they clammed up.

I grew up without the internet and smartphones. Texting wasn't an option. I was an expert in talking to new people. I do it often and mostly enjoy it. It's also one of the first things we taught our kids to do at a restaurant by ordering their own meals. So let's get into it.

Eek! New people! You're about to…

- Go into a new classroom.

- Apply for a job.

- Go to the doctor's office for the first time alone.

- Meet the parents or the kids.

- Eat alone in a restaurant for the first time. (Oh my! This was scary for me the first time, but now I love it. Bring a book or a journal. It's the best!)

- Schedule an appointment.

- Start attending a new group.

- Etc. etc. etc.

… Now what?

Here are some simple things to start with

1. Make eye contact.

2. Greet people. A simple "hello" and "nice to meet you," are simple and effective. Thank people for the invitation or for showing up. Try not to look too angry if you're having a bad day. Chances are that the person you are greeting has nothing to do with your bad day.

3. Speak up! Tell people your name, loud and clear.

4. Shake hands if applicable. Do this when you are meeting the parents or joining a new group, not necessary when checking in at urgent care or greeting wait staff at a restaurant.

5. Have some "small talk" ready to start conversations. Simple, non-combative questions like, "Do you have weekend plans?" Or talk about the venue you're in. Compliment a home or someone's sweater. Be genuine though, everyone can spot a phony. Ask people about themselves. People want to be seen and heard. Listen to responses, continue to ask more questions or relate with your own story. Try not to "one-up" theirs.

6. If you are in a large group and feel like your time is being overrun by someone or you want to move on to a new group to chat with, you may find a pause in the conversation, and excuse yourself. "Sorry to cut you off, but I need to use the restroom/find my mom/check on my date." Follow through with that.

7. If you are a guest in someone's home for a meal, make sure you are helping to set up or to clear plates. Help with the cleanup. Try asking, "What can I do to help?" Or "let me clear those for you." Wait before eating until someone from the family starts. Why? Well, you don't want to be caught with fried chicken hanging out of your mouth if they say a prayer before they eat. "Wait! I don't pray before dinner at my house," you say. Well, you're a guest. Follow along, bow your head. Allow the family to give thanks without your chewing noises. No one is asking you to convert. You might actually find some peace and calm in this pausing process.

8. When it comes to a job interview, be prepared. Research the company, know what they're all about. Practice some basic questions that you might be asked. For example:

   a. What are your strengths? Yes. You have them. Make a list now.

   b. Why should we hire you?

   c. What are your weaknesses? And for the love of God, do not create a giant list of grievances you have with yourself. Choose one thing you'd like to improve upon and explain how you're working on it.

d. What are your past experiences with work? First job? Be honest, but tell them all the ways you're a responsible human. Organized, good grades, taking care of siblings, chores around the house, etc. if you're applying for your first job.

e. How would you handle an angry customer?

f. How might you communicate when you have a problem with a coworker?

9. When you leave, thank people for their hospitality. Whether it's for inviting you in for an interview or inviting you over for a cookout, people are making time for you. Sometimes spending money to have you there. Gratitude will go a long way.

Practice making eye contact, small talk and interview answers in a mirror. Yes, you'll feel silly, but it will totally help; I promise. Remember, above all, be yourself. Be respectful and authentic. The skill of talking to new people is so important to communication and connection. It's a way for us to practice building confidence in ourselves as well.

PART 3:

Relationship with Our Future and Our World

Dear You,

I am so proud of you. You've gotten through so many struggles and continue to grow and learn about yourself. I admire the pivots and healthy risks you've taken. You are your own role model (and one of mine now, too.)

Love, LP

P.S. Your mantra.. Next Right Thing. xo

Taking a Social Media Break

I glance at the kitchen clock. Forty minutes just screamed by in what felt like seconds. How was it possible that I just lost almost an hour of precious time scrolling Instagram AGAIN? I feel numb, ashamed, and "not enough" all at the same time. I know I'm not alone in this time suck. I've seen it happen to my family, friends, and students.

Social media can be a great way to stay connected to our family and friends. I love to stay up on style trends and follow travel bloggers. But, about a year ago I repeatedly found myself being sucked into hours of mindless scrolling which left me feeling foggy and neglectful or angry and sad, depending on what came across my feed.

According to Psychology Today (February 2020), excessive time on social media can lead to an increased risk of depression and anxiety. It can also lead us to feelings of inadequacy about how we look or what we are doing in our lives. I have felt all of this myself, and social media is addictive. It was created that way. Every time we receive a "like," a share, or a comment, we're getting a hit of dopamine to our beautiful brains. Once I connected the dots and realized how my social media binges were affecting my mental state and physical health and interrupting the real relationships in my life, I knew I needed to make a conscious change.

Any change that we want to have in our lives doesn't magically happen. It takes effort and a little smart goal-setting.

Some ideas:

- Set time limits on your phone. Many phones have screen time notifications that you can set up in settings and there are apps like "Freedom" and "Screen Time" that help you set limits for yourself. It's like allowing yourself to eat four cookies but not the whole package.

- Remove the phone from your space. When I need to do an important task, or I want to be more present, I intentionally leave my phone in a different room, in my purse, or in my desk, silenced. Multi-tasking is a myth and social media slows me down.

- Turn off social media notifications. I don't need all of those distractions all the time. When I purposefully check into those outlets, I'll see updates at that time. The people who need me in real life have my phone number.

- Keep the phone out of the bedroom at night; it's too tempting and distracting. I try to put the phone away after dinner to give my brain a chance to take a break.

- Find your joy. Remember what made you happy when you were little? Find a version of that. Get creative. You don't have to be the next Picasso or John Green, you just have to do things that bring you contentment. Draw, write, bake, play a game, take a walk and let your mind wander.

- Journal. Sometimes we inadvertently use social media to distract us from dealing with the tough parts of life. Get all of those thoughts and feelings out of your head. Writing helps you process your life and can give you clarity.

- Set real intentions about how you want to use social media. Think about why you want to log on and build in times to take breaks. Set timers and stick to them. Make a plan for what you'll do when the timer goes off. I like to plan a physical activity like a quick workout video or make a meal to help make it easier to leave the screen.

- Tell the people you spend time with of your intentions. Ask them to help you to be accountable. Maybe they'll want to do a social media detox with you.

How to Play Like a Child

Have you ever wondered why people encourage children to play? Play fosters many good skills like creativity, communication, empathy/sympathy, and grows the imagination. There's even a company in Britain dedicated to helping other companies grow by reteaching the adults how to play again. (Look up the Playcation Experience sometime!) Play is such an important part of being human, no matter your age.

When I was younger I loved to play make-believe with my brothers and cousins. We had a game called "baby witch" that we would play with my cousin's cat. We pretended we were in a band. (Shout out to the Mandrell Sisters!) We created entire synchronized swimming routines in the water and dance routines on land. I coerced my little brother to play house with me, or to be three different characters in our rendition of Sleeping Beauty. As I got older, my creativity came out in other ways. I wrote stories and performed puppet shows with my friend, Kim, in elementary school. I designed outfits for celebrities and created fashion portfolios. (I'm still waiting for Madonna to ask my opinion on styling for her next big adventure.) I later made some of my own clothes for fun. I went through a jewelry design phase. I've even tried crocheting and making things for my home.

But, somewhere along the line, I forgot how to play in my own world. For me, there were clubs to be a part of or papers to write and practice to go to. Then it was papers to grade, dinners to make and clubs to run. I could still be silly or funny, but those were in small doses. I did not make much time for myself to play. After I had kids, I was more concerned that they were playing. Sure, I could play with the kids once I had them, but I tried to let them lead. Sometimes I even felt like I forgot how to play. How was it that I felt like I FORGOT how to PLAY?

If I had to define play, I would say it is doing an action for the pure joy of doing it. Kids do stuff—play—because it's fun and they can embrace all of the happiness that comes with it.

My friend, Sonja, is excellent at playing, even as a grown-up. She is always the first to jump in the deep end. She always dances with the kids, gets dirty, makes art, and is always up for an adventure. She never worries about looking silly or being embarrassed. I have been afraid of being embarrassed about what I might look like to the world if I were to try something new. I honestly don't think I realized how closed off I was to playing, and to living outside of my comfort zone until I watched someone who was living with her whole body and soul. (Thanks, Sister.)

So, now I try to find inspiration from others and by listening to my own body. I ask for help when I need to be taught something. It's not always easy. Sometimes it takes a bit of a "do it scared" attitude.

Some ways to play as an adult:

- Sign up for a new class that teaches you something fun, like dance or welding.

- Follow a child's lead.

- Put your phone away for a few hours and be present with your own desires.

- Build something.

- Plan and execute an adventure.

- Color—adult coloring books are all the trend!

- Create your own favorite themed day.

- Paint.

- Get out some Legos and build.

- Act out a story.

- Turn up some music and just move your body. The kitchen is my favorite spot.

- Create your own adult recess.

- Go to a playground and play on stuff.

- Go outside and move your body.

- Do silly things in the mirror like make faces, motions, movement, or dance.

- Volunteer for game night at a senior center.

- What did you love to do as a kid? Do that!

- What did you always want to try? Try that!

- Gyms and clubs frequently run free or cheap trial memberships. Try one!

- Create a fun persona for a day… Dress up and spend the day in character.
- Watch a funny movie and belly laugh.
- Go to a comedy club.
- Get a group of friends together for a soccer game in the park.
- Go fishing or kayaking.
- Play in the sand.
- (Re)Discover your playful intimate side with your bed partner.

The point of all of this is to feel unproductive and happy with zero agenda. Think of a friend that you have that plays well… What would they do? Better yet, call them and hang out. Take a break from your never-ending to-do list. Or ADD PLAY to your to-do list. Either way, play.

Words Matter

Manners: that's how we function in polite society. It lets people know we appreciate and care about the tasks they're doing for us. Like saying, "please and thank you." It's an acknowledgment of someone's presence. Like, "hello and goodbye."

When I was young, please and thank you were the first phrases I was taught to speak. When my own children were learning to speak, these were also their first phrases. They were taught to use these phrases with everyone, not just family and friends, but cashiers, waitstaff, and daycare providers. Anytime anyone helped them, handed them something, or bought them a gift, they were taught to say "thank you." When they needed something, "please." When entering a room, acknowledge people there. They were taught to shake hands and introduce themselves when meeting new people or seeing someone they hadn't seen in a while. With much practice, these things became routine, natural, and easy to do. But it takes practice and diligence in teaching. As parents, we had to stick with it, reminding them frequently until it became natural. (And as I write this, my sister-in-law texted me that my teenage son is "...so sweet and polite. He already thanked me for his birthday gift." Parenting win.)

So, why do we do this? Why do we greet strangers when we approach or leave them? It's a sign of respect. We are humans, sharing time and space together, working together for the betterment of each other, making our survival here a little easier and more pleasant. Civility is respect for the social contract—the agreement that we will be decent with one another.

Recently, an old friend from high school posted a story on her Facebook page about her thirteen-year-old daughter. The young lady has an ADHD diagnosis and according to her mother, some impulsivity issues that they are dealing with. The young lady can sometimes come across as obnoxious to others, including her classmates. She has a Snapchat account, and she posted a picture to which some of her classmates responded with some of the worst words.

Telling her to kill herself.

Telling her the world wouldn't miss her and might be better without her.

Hurtful words full of venom. She tried to take her life and fortunately she was not successful. She has a supportive family and is getting help.

Although this is her story, it's all too common among so many. It's heartbreaking. And in all of my years in education, this isn't new. Social media just seems to strengthen the bully mentality. And sometimes it ends in a tragedy.

I want to put a couple of reminders out there:

- If you are a student, pay attention to your intentions in the world.

- If you are a parent, remind your kiddos of how to treat others and continue to remind them.

- Talk about and learn from stories like this.

- Know that you are not a burden. You matter.

You do not have to be best friends with everybody you meet. You do not have to go on a date with somebody who is your lab partner in biology. You don't even have to accept everybody's friend request on Instagram or Snapchat or whatever. But what you do need to do is be respectful.

You might not like everybody you come across. Some people are mean and rude. Some people are immature and obnoxious. Some people just rub you the wrong way. But just because somebody isn't exactly your flavor, it does not give you permission to be rude. If you don't have anything kind to say, keep your mouth shut.

If you find yourself in a position where you need to speak up for somebody who is hurting, and that might be yourself, do it with class and grace. Do not stoop to the level of the perpetrator. And remember, you can always walk away. Find your tribe, your ring of protection and speak up for help. It's there. You're not alone.

So, here's the thing: We can either choose to help and make it nicer for the people we encounter, or we can make it harder.

Have you ever worked retail, or been in food service? When you start an interaction with a nice greeting and a client thanks you for your help after requesting something with a "please," everyone feels better in their hearts. When your heart is happy, your brain sends oxytocin into your body, and you feel better. And feeling better just makes existing better. Life isn't easy. We don't need to intentionally make it worse.

Stay Curious and Brave

I don't like that old saying, "curiosity killed the cat." It's stifling. It tells us not to ask questions. It actually kills our curiosity. Questioning and learning are what make us grow and thrive. I'm not just talking about academics here. I'm talking about living your life and exploring what lights you up.

When I was little, I loved to read fiction. Give thirteen-year-old LaRissa some *Sweet Valley High* or anything by Mary Higgins Clark and I was a happy girl. Fast forward to forty-something LaRissa. I teach in a high school; I created and implemented a mentoring program for teen girls (shout out to the Lotus Project!) and I still love true crime. What I was curious about when I was young is still what I'm curious about now. It just looks a little bit different. As I continue to grow, I continue to be more and more curious, and information is so much easier to come by than it was twenty years ago. Thank you, Internet search bar! Sometimes it's like going down a rabbit hole and getting lost like Alice in Wonderland.

The biggest issue I see isn't our lack of access to what we are curious about, it's our lack of bravery in stepping forward into the unknown. Sometimes we don't feel worthy of the adventure or the dream because we've believed some lie that it isn't for us. Or we believe the lie that because no one in our family has done it before, it doesn't feel possible. Or if it doesn't happen quickly for us, it's not ours to enjoy. These are the lies we tell ourselves. And let me fill you in here, no one knows everything. So, the pressure is off. Stop applying all that pressure to yourself. If you don't know something? Ask. Ask the Internet, ask someone you know, ask strangers you don't know. But be brave enough to ask and get curious.

When I was young, I was super curious about Paris. I read books about France, I learned about the people, the food, the culture, and the history. I sought out fiction that took place there. I even took four years of French in high school. I started building a mental map of Paris when I was eight years old. Curious might be an understatement; I was obsessed. If you ask my husband, I still am. It was always my dream to go to Paris and travel abroad to places I had only ever read about in books.

I was thirty-nine the first time I traveled abroad. I had opportunities to travel abroad before that time, but never took the steps to do it or to even try. Unfortunately, there were many lies that I told myself that prevented me from living my dream for so long. Things like…

- It's too expensive and I'll never have the money.
- I should spend the money on other things.
- I should spend my vacation time with my boyfriend who was serving our country instead of doing something for myself. (Sidenote: I did not marry this boy, but I do wish him well.)
- I'm not smart enough to get around a new city.
- Planes are scary and crash all the time.
- Foreign languages are scary.
- I'm too fat to blend in.
- I might not blend in and they'll know I'm an American tourist.
- I might have a bad time.
- I might get lost.
- I might get pickpocketed.
- I don't speak French.
- I have bills to pay and it's not worth my money.
- I'm not fancy enough. (Such a lie, I am totally fancy.)
- People will call me uppity, think I'm wealthy and make fun of me for traveling.
- People will wonder if I've gone into debt for this.
- I shouldn't leave my kids at home.
- I don't have a passport.
- I have nothing to wear in Paris.

Here's why that litany was bad news: it was fear-based. I had to change my mindset and my inner dialogue before I allowed myself to really make my dreams a goal and then a reality. I had to research all the ways to make this happen in a way that worked for me and my family. I had to work for all of that. I had to say and believe:

- I can save money by not buying things that I don't need at the mall.

- I can set money aside before spending it.

- I can work a side hustle to get more cash flow.

- My dreams don't have to be like someone else's.

- Millions of people fly every day. Statistics show us it's safer than cars!

- This trip will give me and my husband an adventure to bond over.

- Paris will not disappoint.

- I am worth this trip.

So, once we decided to go, we saved up for it. I had to research how much it would cost, where we could stay, options for what we would do, and what I should wear. I had to figure out who would watch the kids, and we even updated our will a few months prior to the big trip. I asked a lot of questions… To Google, to Pinterest, and to people I knew who had traveled before. Being curious had never felt so good because curiosity was leading to adventure and catching my dream.

I had to take the same concepts and attitudes when I wanted to design my websites, create blogs, and publish the *Lotus Project* curriculum. I had no idea what I was doing. I had to stay curious, ask questions, and turn down the defeatist negative inner dialog. (Again! Thank you Internet search bar! Thank you people that went before me and let me pick their brains!) I needed to keep a positive mindset. And when I didn't, I needed to remind myself that I was good enough to try. I was inquisitive enough to follow tutorials, attend workshops, and learn how to do things on my own.

I think now, being curious about life is what makes life so good. Sometimes it's just knowing something new; like a documentary about tiny creatures. Sometimes it turns into an action or an adventure; where can I hike near the lake shore? Sometimes it turns into a job; I'm going to ask for a job application or I'm going to start my own online service.

And sometimes it takes you to Paris. And Paris does not disappoint.

Travel Often for Your Well-Being

I've always been a reader. As a kid, books sent me to far away places and times that I could only dream about. Sometimes I went back in time, sometimes I experienced life from another person's shoes, sometimes I saw something new but in my own mind. Growing up, these books gave me an outlet and a place to build empathy. *To Kill a Mockingbird, The Alchemist, Go Ask Alice, The Secret Life of Bees,* and so many more helped shape me.

Being a reader led to me dreaming big dreams of travel and adventure. I had romanticized all of these far away cities, while also being scared of the reality of the unknown. My family did not have the money growing up for big vacations, and as an adult, I didn't know where to start or who to ask. And part of me was just, well, scared.

Eventually, I took these dreams of adventure into my own hands and decided to just GO. It also helped that after I got married, my husband and I found that we travel well together. The first time I took a big road trip it was with my friend, Stacy, to visit my sailor boyfriend in Connecticut. It was a twelve-hour trip that ended up taking us forty-eight hours because we were trying to beat a snow-storm. (Note: Do NOT ever try to beat a snow-storm. It never works out. You end up sleeping in Sbarro's booths on the New York thruway and driving through shady parts of Canada in a delirious sleep-deprived state.) This was before GPS. (Can you imagine a time such as this!?) We printed our directions out at the computer lab from MapQuest and had to frequently cross reference that with our paper atlas. Once we got to our destination, we had to figure out where to get food, find a hotel, call our parents, and decide what to do with our time. After a few days, we had to have the adventure again, but in reverse. And minus the blizzard, thank goodness.

Was this the best trip ever? No. Was it worth it? Absolutely. The work, the stress, the planning, the dealing with the unknown… it showed me that I could do new and hard things! I gained confidence in myself. It helped solidify a friendship that has lasted decades and has blessed me with goddaughters. It showed me the kindness of humanity through the help of strangers. It encouraged me to have more adventures. It made me want to see more of the world for myself.

Having an adventure with a seasoned traveler helps, too. One spring break in college, I flew to Florida with my cousin, Natalie, to visit my other cousin, Amie. She helped me pack a little lighter and navigate the airport a little more smoothly. I still use her methods today. There is also something about a solo trip to help you recharge and gain some confidence, too. After a week of teacher training in London, I spent two days navigating the city alone. As I edit this book right now, I'm alone in a hotel in Chicago. Navigating on your own, without the responsibility of looking after the needs and happiness of others is very liberating. I wouldn't like it all of the time, but every once in a while, it's a good recharge.

Traveling has opened my eyes to so much of the world, but it has also opened my heart to become more loving to myself and to others. First, the sense of accomplishment one feels when navigating a new transit system is a real boost to the confidence monster. Losing your cell signal and relying on your trusted map reminds you that you're a smart, successful adult. Sometimes in life, we just go about our normal activities, and we don't challenge ourselves. We become stagnant and bored. Traveling sets up new challenges for us as a reminder that we don't have to be on that hamster wheel that life sometimes finds us on. Traveling reminds us of our power to be adventurous. And by seeing how others live, you increase your own choices about careers, location, shopping, etc. You see that there are alternative ways to be in this world.

No Growth without Failure

Once upon a time, I applied for a new position within my school district. I spent hours and days prepping, creating, and getting coached up for my interview and presentation. I felt confident that I would do a great job in this new role. I felt ready. I answered the questions well in the interview. I had envisioned a new future for myself, and it felt really good! And I didn't get the job.

I was disappointed. With one phone call, the dreams I had for the upcoming school year went up like a puff of smoke. I grieved for a bit. (This is a really important step.) Then I wished the winner well and moved on. She's a friend and I wanted the program to do well with her at the helm. I thought about things I could have done differently in the interview. I thought of things I could do professionally to better myself moving forward. Yes, I was disappointed but it wasn't the end of the world.

Failure comes in a lot of forms... job applications, tests, Monopoly, sports and even relationships. Sometimes we see failure as the end; the kick-us-when-we're-feeling-down moment. Failure isn't fun, this is true, but it's not the end. It's the lesson.

As a culture, we need to stop this if-I-fail-I-quit attitude and change our mindset. We need to build resilience. Have your moment of disappointment and acknowledge it. Then move on in a positive way.

My brother was playing Monopoly with my son over winter break. My son lost and was pretty annoyed. (The kid is used to beating our entire family at this game.) After the defeat, my brother said to him, "You lost but you need to learn from your opponent." They played again (so many hours of Monopoly!) and the second time my son gave my brother a run for his money. (Pun intended.) He still lost, but was learning the lesson that comes with failure... growth.

Ask yourself some questions:

- What did I do well?

- What can I learn from the experience? (What can I learn from my opponent?)

- What steps can I take next?

With my failure and reflection, I learned some things about interviewing. For me, I also realized that I might not have been ready for this new gig at this stage in my career. I have taken a look at doing new things in my classroom that I am proud of. I started working hard to get the Lotus Project out into the world. I would not have had time for these things with a new job. In hindsight, I'm glad for the interview experience and glad that I'm where I'm at and progressing from here.

Success feels good and boosts confidence, but it doesn't teach you anything new. Failure means I TRIED. It was a brave act. Remember that.

"Smart" Goals and Words to Affirm

At the start of a new year, many of us make resolutions. These can be okay. They force us to reflect on things we'd like to change and start doing things we think will get us where we want to be. Most resolutions are like goals, but they're not goals. They generally don't have a clear path to results and often just set us up for failure after we get bored of the gym by March.

When it comes to a New Year's resolution, many of us strive to do better with our physical bodies. We want to lose weight, work out more, lose weight, eat better, lose weight, lose weight, and lose weight. While losing weight can improve overall health if you are overweight or obese, losing weight is not the end all and be all of YOUR VALUE. Too often we obsess on this area in front of the little kids in our life. (Whether it's a younger sibling, our child, cousin, neighbor...it doesn't matter.) And they are listening. When we have a lot of negative self-talk, it impacts how our kids see us and eventually how they will feel about themselves. This applies to everyone, not just women. It can impact how we see each other. It can lead to unrealistic expectations in the future. The insane expectations that society has put upon each gender for the other can be overwhelming and unobtainable. If we expect to have perfection in each other as well as ourselves, we are setting ourselves up for failure. And when we tell ourselves these unobtainable lies, it gets under our skin, and we start to believe these things are our value.

Instead of focusing on the skinny-ripped-hot version of yourself, focus on the HEALTHY version. Talk about how working out gets your heart pumping better. Plan healthy meals to help your brain focus more. Talk about the STRENGTH you have in your thighs. Encourage your kids to do activities with you while discussing a long and healthy life to play in. (And if you want to be a hot ripped bodybuilder and creating that body brings you joy—then do it. But do it because you enjoy that, not because you feel like it is something required of you.)

Here's the thing about goals. You first need to think about WHAT you want to achieve and reflect on WHY you want to achieve that. Really listen to yourself and understand your "why." How will you feel if you are successful? What if you're not? Take some time in your own head. Ask yourself tough questions.

Once you have a goal in mind, be SMART about it... Specific-Measurable-Actions-Realistic-Time (accountability)

> SPECIFIC—Be precise when setting a goal. Don't just say you're going to pass your classes or make more money, be specific.

Try this: You're going to set a study schedule and ask for help to pass your classes. You're going to update your resume, go to local networking parties, ask for a raise, etc.

> MEASURABLE—The goal needs to be something you can have control over. Winning the lottery is out of your control. That's not a realistic goal. (But, if you get lucky, KUDOS!)

Try this: Don't just say, I'm going to go on a vacation. Try, I am going to save $20 out of every paycheck to put toward my vacation.

> ACTIONS—Create a list of actions that you will need to do to obtain your goal.

Try this: If your goal is to start a blog, research and write down what you need to do to start that. You will have a long list of action items that can then be broken down into smaller obtainable pieces.

> REALISTIC—Goals should be challenging but not impossible. You need to start with "baby steps" to get mentally prepared. I was once told that a goal should be "out of your reach but within your grasp." Make your goal not so easy that you do it immediately but not so challenging that you will have no chance of being successful.

Try this: Instead of telling yourself you are going to write a book, make a list of the steps you'd like to start with. Brainstorm topics, buy a notebook to start writing in (or create a new Google Doc), schedule time every week for yourself to write… these are the start of the baby steps you'd need.

> TIME—Make a calendar, hold yourself accountable. Better yet, have a friend help you stay accountable. There's power in numbers!

Try this: Take your action items (above) and put them into three categories, immediate, mid-term, and long-term. Start by scheduling the time on your calendar for your immediate goals first. Then move on from there.

If you would like my personal organizer and goal setting guide, check this out: https://www.thelotusproject.net/product-page/personal-organizer

GOAL SETTING
plan

GOAL	START DATE:	END DATE:

Turn dreams into goals...

ACTION STEPS

POSSIBLE OBSTACLES

HOW TO OVERCOME OBSTACLES

Magical Phrase

As I grew older, I came to realize that my mindset was what needed to change. Instead of creating resolutions that weren't reasonable, I started setting SMART goals. Creating these goals allowed me to take baby steps and make changes in a healthy way, any time of the year, not just in January. I found much more success. But now, I give myself an annual word or phrase to remind me of the direction I want to be headed. It became like a mantra. A personal positive reminder. I love my "words of the year" and look forward to setting them every winter or every birthday.

A few years ago, it was "Be Brave." I chose this because I realized I was unintentionally taking the easy and comfortable way, with my business and my job. I always made the "safe bet." I was afraid of failing and was not taking healthy risks. So "Be Brave" helped push me to make some out-of-my-comfort-zone decisions and it was so helpful.

Last year, my phrase was "Learn and Grow." I was frustrated that I couldn't do it all, all at once. I was losing patience with myself, and I also felt overwhelmed with the resources available to me. There was so much to do! So much new material to try to utilize! "Learn and Grow" helped me to realize that it was a good thing to pause, to take a class, and educate myself in order to grow my business or do some self-improvement. It helped remind me that life is a journey and change isn't usually instantaneous, but requires hard work, education, and dedication.

Carve out some time on your calendar to gain some clarity on these focus words. Maybe near your birthday or the last week in December. Put it in your calendar and block time. Get a babysitter or go to a library or cafe. Turn off your phone. Take your time and really dig deep. Set a ten to fifteen-minute timer, free write and flow. Some questions to ask yourself:

- What do I do well?

- What changes would I like to see?

- How do you hold yourself back?

- What positive messages resonate with you most?

And if you're feeling a little stuck on figuring out your magical phrase, maybe these will inspire you.

If your inner dialogue is negative, how about...

- I have a gift.

- Strength and honor.

- No mind bullies.

If you're in a state of overwhelm...

- I am enough.

- Strong and resilient.

- Next right thing.

If you always feel like you should be doing everything like everyone else...

- Should is a shame word.

- Stop shoulding on yourself.

If you keep drawing in toxic people and things...

- Break away.

- I'm worth better.

If you're in need of positive reinforcement...

- Lead with love.

- Do it scared.

- Be brave.

- I'm tough.

Choose something that fits with you best! Nobody knows you the way you know yourself. Take some time to get into your head to remind yourself of what you really need. Sometimes we need to be our own fairy godmother and it starts with a healthy reminder.

Epilogue

Everytime I had someone look at this book, even small parts, I felt like throwing-up. I don't know if I've ever felt so vulnerable in my life.

While I was writing, I was excited to share my thoughts and ideas. I worked hard, and I thought I was ready. Then, the book was finished. It was time for the next steps in the process. And all I wanted to do was quit. I was terrified of anyone reading it and hating it. Writing is so personal, especially when you're writing about your own life. And then those negative thoughts started running through my head… *If someone reads it and hates it, would that mean they hate me, too? I'm not a trained author - why am I writing a book? I have nothing to say that people haven't heard, so why would anyone read this? This book is trash.*

Yes, even the gal writing the book that talks about self love, positive mindset, and using your voice was listening to the negative self talk that naturally popped into her head.

Then, another - louder, more persistent - voice jumped in. It was the inner cheerleader, the teacher, the wise part; this part had something more important to say. She reminded me to do it scared. I guess I reminded myself. I asked myself what I would tell a friend? I followed my own advice. Here's the thing: it's hard. It's work. It is a constant pause, reflect, reset. Wash, rinse, repeat.

Life is not easy, folks. Being a human full of emotions, challenges and ego is hard to navigate. Trying to improve how we are in this world is hard work. We do not come with a manual. We have to come up with our own. Here's mine.

Acknowledgements

Matthew, thanks for loving me when I was annoyingly riddled with doubt. Thanks for bringing me snacks on the days when I was plugging away and not taking care of myself. Thanks for being the center circus tent pole to my ringmaster of this circus life we've built.

Jack and Mariano, thanks for being the coolest humans, giving the best hugs, and for picking up the extra chores when I was working extra at home. That laundry does not fold itself!

Pamela Gress, thank you for being my first reader and giving me your honest feedback. I want to be like you when I grow up.

Nicole Norburg, thank you for knowing just what to say and when to say it. Our relationship is like balm to my soul.

My tribe of women - I'm blessed that there are too many to list - I'm so lucky to have so many sisters to pour my heart out to! Thanks for supporting my shenanigans and for loving me when I wasn't loving myself.

Audrey Shantz, I feel like I've known you for decades. Thank you for creating beautiful art and for sharing it with the world.

Krista, you are the best therapist a girl could ever have. Thanks for working with me and helping me grow.

Kate, up in heaven, thanks for being my first hard truth teller. You're in my heart always.

Lisa Anselmo and Gabrielle Luthy, thanks for being the best teachers for authors and for creating not only inspiring books but the Paris Writing Salon.

Rachel Kerr and the editing staff at Book Baby. Thank you.

And finally, this book could not have happened without the love and financial support of the folks that backed my Kickstarter. My heart is still overflowing with gratitude. Thank you.

For more information on the Lotus Project visit thelotusproject.us.

To find the author online check out lpinspire.com or follow her on Instagram and Facebook at @lpinspire.